COOKING ALONE

by the same author

COOKING FROM SCRATCH

COOKING FOR A PARTY

Cooking Alone

KATHLEEN LE RICHE

faber

First published in 1954 by Faber & Faber Limited

This new edition published in the UK and USA in 2021
by Faber & Faber Ltd
Bloomsbury House
74–77 Great Russell Street
London WC1B 3DA

Printed and bound in the UK by CPI Group (UK) Ltd, Croydon CR0 4YY

A CIP record for this book
is available from the British Library

ISBN 978–0–571–36579–1

2 4 6 8 10 9 7 5 3 1

For those who wish to
and those who must
find solace in solitude

FOREWORD BY BEE WILSON

It is easy to underestimate a book like this, which is not only very short but more or less totally forgotten. In all my years of talking about cookbooks, I have never heard anyone describe themselves as a Kathleen Le Riche fan. And yet *Cooking Alone*, first published in 1954, is something remarkable. Aside from its wit and period charm, this is one of the very few cookbooks to recognise that the most important ingredient in the kitchen is the human being who cooks.

The minute you start to flick through, you notice that the book's structure is unique. Instead of dividing up the chapters into types of dishes – starters and main courses or meat, fish and vegetables and so on – Le Riche names her chapters after different types of solitary cooks: an array of human characters. There is The Old Lady who cooks white fish to share with her pets; The Career Woman who feels she deserves a roast chicken now and then; and The Happy Potterer who loves to experiment with unusual flavours such as lamb chop with olives. Each of these characters enables Le Riche to address a different aspect of cooking alone, whether it's the problem of storing ingredients for one without them going to waste (The Bachelor) or the dilemma of keeping equipment to a minimum while still having what you need to produce a satisfying meal (The Bed-Sitter).

The mood of the book is old-fashioned and modern at the same time. Many of the dishes described by Le Riche are from a Miss Marple-ish world of British food that has vanished. Other than a surprising recipe for rabbit with aubergine, there is almost no trace of the sunny French and Italian cooking that Elizabeth David had been writing about since the publication of *A Book of Mediterranean Food* in 1950. Le Riche writes of semolina puddings and liver and bacon, of mutton broth and ways to jazz up a tin of fruit with 'a little cream and a sweet wafer biscuit'. Most of the characters have no fridge. If they want to buy a block of ice cream, they must wrap it in several layers of newspaper to stop it melting.

But while Le Riche's cooking may be old-school, her theme is excitingly current. This is fundamentally a book about self-care. 'Yes, I take care of myself rather well', comments one of the characters. *Cooking Alone* is about ways to be kinder to yourself when you are alone in the kitchen, whatever your reasons for being alone. As Le Riche rightly observes, some choose their solitude as cooks while others have it forced upon them. In either case, the key to enjoying cooking more is to find your own 'positive incentives'. It's also about being realistic. 'Forgive yourself if you have to use margarine instead of butter for frying', she comments in one recipe for fried chicken with 'pimiento', by which she means sweet red pepper.

Le Riche writes perceptively about what it feels like to pay attention to your own appetites. Each of the characters has their own particular hidden passions. The Bed-Sitter is a young man who 'began to dream about cookers – tall, short, handsome, squat, Dutch ovens, boiler-grillers'. The Bachelor is obsessed with vegetables, and finds himself hypnotised by their bright colours at the market 'like a woman at a dress shop window'. The Student makes delicious pikelets for herself on the ring heater in her student digs from a batter that is 'thick like clotted cream'.

Le Riche herself is something of a mystery. I could find out almost nothing about her, except that this was her third cookbook, after *Cooking from Scratch* in 1951 and *Cooking for a Party* in 1953. By the 1960s she seems to have abandoned food writing and become an amateur Shakespeare scholar. A critic for the *Belfast News Letter* praised *Cooking from Scratch* as 'a clever book, and amusing too'. The premise of the book was that Le Riche had started off hating cooking but now found herself an accomplished cook: 'from can-opener to Cordon Bleu!', as the blurb described it.

Whatever her own life story, there is no doubt that Le Riche displays a rare understanding of the psychological obstacles that a person may need to get over to enjoy solitary cooking. This comes out especially strongly in the moving final chapter, 'The Lonely Mother', which is about a woman who spends the day from nine to five alone in her house while her children are at school, yet who often simply doesn't eat because she is so busy with housework. This mother suddenly imagines how different it would be if she were expecting someone else for lunch or tea and resolves to start cooking for herself as generously as if she were her own guest. *Cooking Alone* is ultimately a call to cook for yourself as if you matter. It's sad that, nearly seventy years on, this still feels like a radical message.

Bee Wilson, 2020

CONTENTS

Contents

I

HUNTING THE INCENTIVE

Wherever I go, and whenever I discuss cooking with the people I meet, I find a resistance which is almost general among people who are alone. Whether the solitude is more or less permanent, or a temporary ménage, the attitude is, "I can't be bothered."

The result is too often a devitalized condition which, in itself, breeds inertia and therefore more reluctance to be bothered. The Awful End of this anaemic attitude ought to be incentive enough—to avoid. But there are many more positive incentives to induce one to cook, and enjoy what is cooked. It need not be a fulsome, arduous meal of several courses. Nor need it be a filling kind of snack the filler of which is mostly bread.

From my experience, and that of others who have talked with me, I have found, and here set out, the simple, colourful, nourishing dishes which are adequate, yet easy to prepare.

The characters present their own incentives and ideas about happy eating, among which may be yours.

II

THE OLD LADY

"People are beginning to notice it—the way I talk to myself," she said. "I'll buy myself a canary. Not a cage, though. I'll have netting across the window, and let him free. And I might have a little cat—though she might harm the bird. But I'll have a little dog, so that when I'm out, conversing with myself, people will think my remarks are addressed to whatever is at the end of the string.

"There's no reason why I shouldn't talk to myself.... I find my own articulate thoughts so *interesting*. When anyone visits me and talks . . . I have noticed myself only waiting for them to pause, so that I may continue my own Argument. A little dog wouldn't interrupt me. He'd look at me with his big eyes. And I'd smooth his silky head, and hold his paws so that he wouldn't tear my silken skirt. . . ."

"But you'd have to feed him!"

She hadn't heard the knock on her door; nor had she observed it opening. But there was her neighbour, already informed of her project and her disposition. So they discussed the way the pets should be fed.

He said, "Feed a dog as you feed yourself."

"Do you mean that I should eat horsemeat! Or that I should give him a share of my chicken?"

"Can't see you doing that, old lady. No, what I meant was, cook the meat and the fish and the veg., and make it tasty. Some nice gravy, for your dog."

"But he should have bones."

"Ah, but with plenty on them."

"And biscuits!"

"Hard ones—good for his teeth, like the bones."

"Perhaps I'll have a pusscat."

"Have a peke, and then you'll have a cat and a dog rolled into one."

And so she did. And very soon after that she had a Siamese cat as well, and her conversational powers were well exercised. Indeed it was not the only exercise, because several times a week she was compelled to walk to the butcher, to the fishmonger, to the green as well as the dry grocer. It was a necessity, an objective, an interest and a satisfaction. With the Siamese snugly balanced on her shoulder, keeping her ear warm, and the peke at her heels, or visiting, she felt as important as if she had a family.

Buying their food, she bought also for herself . . . rabbits, stewing steak, large white fish (easy to bone), veal bones (one for the dog and the rest for soup) as well as other meat bones which she gave to him, raw. Sometimes she shared her ice-cream with her fastidious Siamese.

"Having a nice share of the dog's dinner?" Her neighbour poked his head in one day. She liked him; accepted his interest with his knowing ways and the pert comments which came with him, inevitably.

This time he had hit on the very thing she had been thinking. "Have I been talking aloud to myself again?"

"Not this time. But I guessed. It gets like that when you keep pets. You stew the rabbit or the steak, and you keep testing it to see if it's tender. And if it's nice enough for them, it's nice enough for you. . . . And if you've got something you enjoy, you give them a bit, see? Or leave them quite a lot. And watch them eat it!"

"A LITTLE AND OFTEN"

Since she had been growing old she had experienced the truth of what she had often heard—that large meals tax the digestion—so she prepared small portions, eating at two- or three-hourly intervals. Instead of the two- or three-course meal, she ate the meat or a savoury at one time, and later on ate the pudding, the sweetmeat, or the fruit.

She had learned another very important thing about keeping her appetite and her digestion in good working order—she *never ate when she was utterly fatigued*. She rested in quite a relaxed position for at least fifteen minutes before eating or trying to prepare her meal.

"When I've rested—and shopping always tires me—I take a little reviver while I begin to cook," she told me when I called on her. And she showed me her little list, becauses she realizes she is also becoming forgetful.

The Old Lady

REVIVERS

A spoonful of honey, or Blackcurrant purée, Apple jelly or Rosehip syrup.

A wineglassful of orange squash, undiluted, Grapefruit squash, or Tomato juice with a spot of Worcestershire sauce, all very cold.

A few nuts, sultanas, or boxed dates.

Best of all: two lumps of sugar.

HERBAL TEA is a great reviver—the green leaf maté tea, the dried lime blossoms, camomile daisies or elderflower —a few spoonfuls left to infuse for ten minutes after pouring on boiling water will make several cups. As it retains its flavour and no harm comes to it, it can be kept overnight provided it is strained off the leaves or flowers. It takes only a minute then to re-heat, with or without sugar, but *no* milk.

"No wine, my dear!" she says. "Not at my age while I cook. I should simply drop off to sleep. But I like a little tipsy cake."

TIPSY CAKE

"I buy a portion of sponge cake with cream sandwiched in it, and put it on my most beautiful plate. It always gives me pleasure to eat from what remains of my exquisite china. I pour a wineglass of sherry over the cake (or brandy or rum) and cover it with a dish while I'm eating my savoury course, perhaps. By the time I'm ready for my tipsy cake it is well saturated, squashy and luscious."

FRESH FRUIT CAKE

"A fresh fruit cake is another thing I like. I buy a fresh, plain sponge cake and keep it in an airtight tin, taking a slice from it as I need it. This I split through the middle and arrange in it, like a sandwich, sliced peeled pear, peach, apricot, or any of the soft fruits in season, such as raspberries or strawberries. Even tinned fruits will do, of course—the crushed pineapple is very good—and I pour over the cake and the fruit the cream from the top of my milk. Or I might buy a little pot of cream, or yoghourt which needs caster sugar or honey on it to modify the rather tart flavour."

SPONGE CAKE

"Often I prefer to make my own sponge cake, for which I use my cake tin with a tube through the middle, so that there's never any question about the centre sagging. And I use two eggs to make it light and airy, avoiding the need of much baking powder which I rather dislike.

"First I drain the whites out of the eggs into a dry basin. I stand another basin containing two ounces of margarine with three ounces of sugar, in a bowl of hot water to melt, and mix the egg yolks into this melted cream until all is smooth. I sift three heaped tablespoonfuls of plain flour with half a teaspoonful of salt, then sift it again into the cream, mixing it by lifting to keep it airy. When I have it I grate into that the zest (rind) of an orange or a lemon, using the juice to mix the dough—just enough to make it soft. When I have no fruit I mix it with a little warm milk or evaporated milk.

"The egg whites must be whisked up till they resemble firm snow, and spooned into the dough at the very last, just before it is ready to be cooked. This makes a dough almost as softly fluid as a thick batter. So I scoop it into my cake tin which I've greased slightly, shaking a little caster sugar over it to create that crystalline look, and let it bake at a moderate heat, about 400° F. or mark 6 if one cooks by gas.

"It is cooked in about half an hour, when it will be light gold in colour and will be springy when you touch the top. So I take it out and invert it over a wire mesh, and, as it cools, it releases itself from the tin, which I lift off to let the steam free. When it is quite cold and settled I enclose it in my airtight tin, not before."

ICING

"Sometimes I ice my slice. A dessertspoonful of sifted icing sugar is mixed in a cup containing a drop of water or milk, over hot water, until it is fluid—it takes one minute —and it is ready to pour over the cake on the plate."

She went on talking of her inventive ideas for quite a time, words and gestures presenting a vivid picture out of the back of her mind. But she had long been unaware of my presence, so I left her, happy, absorbed, eloquent; and I shut the door.

III

THE BACHELOR

When I saw him standing at the greengrocer's shop, then hovering a few steps farther on at the fishmonger's, then back again to the piled fruit and vegetables, hypnotized like a woman at a dress shop window, I knew he was an inveterate shopper. As she would be saying to herself, "How ravishing is that amethyst velvet; how well it would light up my raven hair! Or that black figured satin which I could wear with one pearl ornament . . . just one!" So he, unable to resist that radiant display of bright colours, would remain within the orbit of fresh celery, newly boiled beetroots, grapefruits, crisp apples and clean-washed parsnips until he bought . . . just one! of each, and a carrier to put them in as well as the fish from next door. So, carrying them away covetously, he would only remember when he was at his own doorstep that his small kitchen was already overflowing with these irresistible things—some beginning to rot.

So the debate would begin. "Must eat the older ones first. . . . No, let's have the fresh ones while they are fresh, NOW", and the rest would sadden and yawn for their overdue repository—the rubbish bin. It was only after some months of living alone, that he was able to organize his domestic habits so that he lived well, hygienically and without waste.

STORING

Storing what he had bought was his main problem, solved in this way:

BREAD was bought in a waxed paper wrapping, or rolled in a linen cloth so that it could "breathe".

GREEN VEGETABLES were washed (the coarse outer leaves discarded) and drained, then piled in a plastic bowl, covered with a damp linen cloth.

STALKS LIKE CELERY were stood in a jar, half filled with water. In the same way he kept parsley fresh.

ROOT VEGETABLES were kept on an airy wire rack. "Keep your powder dry" was his watchword for FLOUR, which keeps best in its cotton bag. The other cereals such as RICE and BARLEY he kept in screw-top glass jars.

SPICES he kept in jars also, so that the contents were visible.

BISCUITS were kept crisp, and CAKES were kept moist in separate air-tight tins, as were the different varieties of SUGAR, TEA and COFFEE.

DRIED FRUITS, because of their acid content, corroded the tins, so they had to be stored in glass jars with waxed paper lids, or covers of imitation porous skin.

Through such foresight, the mice never bothered him, as they too often do when their journeys are rewarded by finding food uncovered or in paper bags which they nibble through.

He bought strings of ONIONS from the ingratiating Breton boys, and hooked them up behind his kitchen door with a bag of DRIED HERBS. The mice, so far, had not been attracted by this fare.

The MILK, CHEESE, MEAT and FISH had to be considered quite seriously, so he decided to invest in a little safe which keeps food stone-cold by simply standing a dish of fresh water inside at the top.

Until then, he stood the butter and the bottle of milk on separate dishes, put an earthenware cover over each and poured cold water over that morning and night. The water evaporating caused the chilling. During hot weather if the milk had to be kept overnight, he scalded it—brought it up to bubbling point—then poured it into a cold jug, stirred it and covered it with muslin to keep the flies out. In the summer-time he often bought the sterilized milk with the "crown" cap which keeps its fresh flavour for three or four days. It is so good to make milk puddings with, giving them a rich, creamy colour. It is very nice in coffee, too, but is ruinous in tea. And because it won't clot it is no use trying to make it into a junket, for which fresh milk only may be used.

This was the end of all garbage hoarding, and not a fly was to be seen.

His accommodation was lavish, he was told, though it seemed to him skimpy enough, "But what", said his friend, "if you had only a bed-sitter, like mine?"

IV

THE BED-SITTER

"Are you really a bed-sitter, or is it that you rent a bed-sitter?"

"In truth it is a studio. Not that I paint. But it is large enough for all the functions," said he. "In one corner I sleep, in another I dine, in another I have my desk for work and in the fourth I cook."

"And wash up?"

"Fortunately there is an offshoot with a bath and washing facilities. But my cooking equipment is arranged around and under my table cooker, all quite decently concealed, as you see, by that rather smart washable curtain."

Against the wall was a wooden kind of plaque screwed with many pegs like a dart-board for the things which can hang, and in a white-wood cupboard were the things which stood. The minimum needs he counted carefully.

EQUIPMENT

A strong steady TABLE with smoothly running drawers for cutlery and linen, with a projecting edge on which can be screwed a mincer, vegetable peelers, etc., and on which may be safely stood a TABLE COOKER, whether gas or electricity; these are now made conveniently with a boiler-griller top and tiny oven, so that the food on cooking plates or dishes can be made hot over the top and under it without wasting any heat. See *Note* page 24.

A metal COLD SAFE for storing quickly perishable foods.

A plastic BOWL—dirt resistant and unbreakable, in which to wash vegetables, mix dough, and for washing up.

Strong SAUCEPAN with two short handles, for use over the heat and inside the oven as a casserole dish.

COLANDER with graduated base to fit various sizes of saucepans.

GLASS LID that is a dinner plate with a graduated base to fit any pan and which is thus made hot—ready to eat from.

Fireproof glass, enamel *which does not chip*, or earthenware DISHES:

One shallow, which can be used over the heat and under the grill, from which food may be eaten.

One deep dish for cooking larger quantities.

CASSEROLE of clear oven glass, with wide lips to grip, and without food-trapping ridges.

MEASURING JUG and a BASIN for mixing.

TIN OPENER.

CORKSCREW.

CROWN BOTTLE CAP OPENER.

NUTCRACKERS.

KNIVES with blades running right through the handles and riveted, not glued on at the hilt, and all stainless:

One long for carving meat and slicing bread.

One short, very sharp and pointed for vegetable peeling.

One short and serrated for shredding vegetables, slicing slippery things like tomatoes and other fruits.

One wide and flexible for lifting and scooping.

A perforated EGG or FISH SLICE for lifting, turning and draining foods.

Strong, stainless SCISSORS.

Strong FORK for mixing dough and batters.

EGG WHISK.

STRAINERS—stainless, and cast in one piece, thus eliminating the usual dirt trap at the join. A large one for sieving flour, making fruit or vegetable purée. A small, fine one for straining tea or coffee.

Flat open-backed GRATER.

Stainless LADLE for lifting and transferring anything fluid—soups, stewed fruits, jams, drinks.

Flat wooden CHOPPING BOARD, (reversible) for bread, pastry and vegetables.

Flat-ended WOODEN SPOON and MEASURING SPOONS.

PASTRY ROLLER.

Enamelled or plastic TRAY for every kind of purpose

BRUSHES for cleaning vegetables and dishes.

Folding PLATE RACK for dripping dishes.

Enamelled or plastic washable REFUSE BIN.

Nylon woven PAD and a MOP for dish washing.

This seemed an exhaustive list for a bed-sitter, but lack of an adequate implement could inhibit him from cooking at all, so that, impatiently, he would go out to eat and spend more than he had intended. Besides it amused him to try out various gadgets. A new one spurred him to fresh cooking experiments when his interest had flagged.

In time he acquired a long-handled SANDWICH TOASTER, a COFFEE GRINDER, which he screwed to the back of his door, the GLASS COFFEE-MAKER which can be put directly upon heat, a MEAT MINCER, screwed to the table, a ROTARY GRINDER for nuts and cheese, a PEPPER MILL, a VEGETABLE PEELER, a POTATO CHIPPER, a PRESSURE COOKER, and a "ticker timer" MINUTE CLOCK which he could set for the prescribed cooking-time and so occupy himself otherwise until recalled by the ping of the bell.

Eventually he gained quite a reputation among his friends as an admirable host, though he always practised with every gadget and every dish at first *quite alone*.

THE COOKER

Note: Before bed-sitting with a table cooker, he had to give it quite a deal of thought. Safety, competence, space, appearance and cost he considered, in that order.

SAFETY

GAS. Provided he didn't turn on a gas tap inadvertently, or that the wind didn't blow the flame out when he wasn't paying attention, thereby accumulating unburned gas, it was safe to strike a match (or the patent lighter) to light the cooker. Any gas escape announces itself by the smell, so, having a sensitive nose, he was well armed against possible accident. Kitchen cloths, or any clothing which could wave in a breeze, would have to be watched, as well as spitting fat under the grill, in case the flame flared up. A similar precaution would have to be taken in the case of toasting bread in front of the gas fire—if the bread became alight by holding it too close.

The gas connection must be fitted by a skilled and responsible person, and all tubing must be tested carefully for possible leakages.

ELECTRICITY. An electric fire, unprotected by a guard, was also a danger, he knew. Any jab through with a fork or other metal implement he might be holding which touched the naked, live element might cause a short circuit, even a shock, especially if one were standing on a stone floor or a wet one. The naked element, which is the finely coiled wire, is exposed on a fire and on the kind of grill which is covered by a SOLID HOT-PLATE. There are protecting meshes or rods, but, even if unlikely, it is possible for a metal instrument to get through and touch it. It is better therefore, *always*, to pull a grill pan away from under the heat while turning the food.

A RADIANT PLATE, however, has its element enclosed entirely in a metal tube. This tube is formed into an open zig-zag or twirl, and the reflector underneath causes the red-hot glow to shine upwards. If the reflector is placed over the tubing, the glow shines downwards. A saucepan poised above the hot-plate also sends the heat down, while becoming hot itself. By this means there is a saving of heat—one plate for grilling and boiling which is safe. A radiant plate becomes hot very quickly, whereas a solid plate takes a time to become really hot. If there is a naked element underneath it, however, this becomes red-hot very quickly indeed. On no account should one cook *over* a naked element if one seeks absolute safety.

Whichever type of electric cooker one chooses, the essential thing is to have it earthed; that is, to have it fitted with a three-point plug, and have the three wires fixed to it by an expert, never by an amateur. Also the power or light point to which it is connected must be adequate, and the cable or flex must be entirely insulated and securely placed where it cannot be trodden on or caught with the foot or other object.

Having absorbed these elementary points concerning safety, he felt free to take into account the other questions in his head, commenting to himself that it is always dangerous to play with fire!

CHOOSING

After some exploration among so many kinds, he began to dream about cookers—tall, short, handsome, squat, Dutch ovens, boiler-grillers, waterless cookers, breakfast cookers, baby ovens—all the kinds that end in "ette". But always he was baffled by the unnecessary food-trapping crevices.

When his brain had cleared, he chose! He bought a boiler-griller (with a hot-cupboard for plates and a wide top to stand pans on), the heat of which could be controlled and graduated.

The Bed-Sitter

Later on he bought a portable, shining oven, the heat of which remained steadfast so that he could neither hurry a dish nor spoil it, and which confined the juices and the smell entirely. It was surprisingly cheap.

V

THE HAPPY POTTERER

"I adore pottering", she said, "and there's no one left to stop me." Her brothers used to call her "Andfauna" just because she was christened something that went with it. "But brothers always tease, don't you know," she would say good-humouredly, watering her window-box of herbs —chives, thyme, lemon thyme, sage, mint, a trailing nasturtium,—even parsley which is a petulant plant.

"I like to have everything at hand, so that I can suit my dish to my whim. Perhaps I am rather whimsical. I spend as much as half an hour sometimes preparing my coffee— grinding it, infusing it, filtering it, or percolating it, whipping the cream—just as I fancy. But I'm forgetful. That's why I've written out the various dishes I make from time to time—just in case I wander off to do something else. A descriptive recipe keeps me to heel as it were. Not that I stop inventing. I always do something a little differently. But I *enjoy* it—preparing my food—and, for the first time in my life My Time Is My Own. No one hustles me. The clock can stop, for all I care."

"How do you know it's meal time?"

"By my hunger. I never munch intermittently; I mean indiscriminately. I wait, sometimes hours, I'm sure. I become absorbed in reading, or walking or sewing—something, or re-arranging things—just pottering, especially in my sunny little kitchen. Would you like to borrow my book of words? Really, you can have it. I'll soon make another."

So I quote freely from her collection of recipes which are pinned together in an envelope marked "Sur Le Plat" —to be cooked on the plate, which must be one which can be used over the heat, and under the grill, to cook top and bottom.

LAMB CHOP AND OLIVES, WITH TOAST

Turn on the grill. Cut away the thick fat from the chop with scissors. Chip it up and put it on the fireproof shallow dish to melt as the heat mounts. Peel a clove of garlic; cut it up on the lean of the chop on a separate plate. Sprinkle lemon juice or vinegar over it, too. Turn it over and do the same. When the grill is red-hot, dip sliced bread in the melted fat and leave it on the plate. This absorbs the surplus and stops much splutter. Put the lean chop on the hot fireproof dish with the melted fat, and half a dozen black olives, under a red-hot grill. Turn the chop after one minute to let it brown. Turn it again once or twice until it is cooked through. Don't overcook or it will be hard. When it is nearly done, put the soaked bread on top and let it toast. Turn it to toast the other side, so that it will be crisp *dripping toast*. By that time the chop will be cooked.

Eating from the dish means one dish and a plate to wash up. As the dish will be so hot, protect the tray or table by putting down a non-slip cork, composition or other heat-resisting mat first. Never neglect this.

SAUSAGES, GHERKINS AND TOMATOES

One can't really buy less than half a pound of sausages, which is too much for me for one meal. Even so, I prefer to cook them all at once. While the grill is becoming hot, prick the sausages with the points of the scissors, all over. This prevents a burst skin.

(Scissors are excellent for gripping hot things and turning them under the grill, provided you don't poke them upwards and touch the naked element if it's an electric grill. Even if it's gas, pull the pan out to do the turning.)

Slice several pickled gherkins, and halve whatever tomatoes you wish to eat. Leave the skin on so that they keep their shape. Set the sausages on the fireproof plate and let them sizzle under the red-hot grill. Turn them, and put the tomatoes and gherkins alongside to become hot. Soak bread in the liquid fat which emerges, and toast it both sides.

DIET

These meals provide the protein (meat, nuts, eggs, or fish), carbohydrate (starch), the warming fats and vitamins with what the Americans call "salts" (vegetables), as well as variations of colour for a balanced meal.

It's easy to remember if you have always something brown, white, green and red. Also yellow, if you can. Make up what is missing by a fruit or creamy sweet course afterwards, or later on in the day. That's all I want to remind myself about *diet* just now.

SAUSAGES FRIED

It's no good trying to fry sausages from the raw. They spit and break asunder. Once they are grilled the way is prepared. Those grilled yesterday are easy to slice, lengthwise, or across in rings. Instead of a frying-pan or frying-plate, I sometimes use a saucepan for shallow frying. Get it quite hot with a lump of dripping or margarine in it. When the fat is really hot, not before, put in the sausages slices. Keep turning them until they are hot right through.

BACON FRIED WITH MUSHROOMS

Fry bacon in a deep pan, too. It confines the spraying fat fumes. Cut the fat off first, and nip the rind here and there with the scissors to prevent it from curling. When it has melted in the saucepan, put in the lean bacon and let it fry in its fat. Keep turning it, but don't wait for it to go brown or it will be as hard as a nutshell. Rub the button mushrooms over with a linen cloth dipped in salt, to clean them. Or rinse the open ones in a bowl of cold water. Don't bother to peel them. Slice them down through the stems and put them in when the bacon is taken out. Keep turning them until they darken, when they will be cooked through. For this dish a plate must be heated separately. Toast bread on it under the grill while the top is being used for the bacon. A bowl of watercress goes very well with this instead of a green cooked vegetable.

BACON GRILLED WITH EGG

When the bacon is grilled it can be made truly crisp. The fat runs off it. Put a piece of bread under it to catch the melting fat, which is afterwards toasted as dripping toast. Take the bacon and the toast off the grilling-plate, which should have enough fat left to cook an egg. If not, add a knob of margarine, slide in the egg and let it grill gently. The hot plate will set the underneath, and the grill will set the top. Put the bacon back to become hot again in a few minutes, and it is ready to eat.

HOT SAUCE

Heat any tomato ketchup you may like to use, when the egg is nearly set, under the grill, or over the top. It is much nicer than putting it on cold, as is usual.

GRILLED STEAK

Sometimes one is lucky and the beef steak is tender as a lamb; soft and finely grained. If so, simply slide it on its dish under a red-hot grill. This will sear it and so seal in the juices which will keep the flavour intact. But do the same the other side in one minute. Turn it with the scissors.

Turn the grill down a little, so that the rest of the cooking may be moderate and penetrating. The tenderness will remain if it is not overcooked. Ten minutes in all should be adequate.

No spot of the escaping juice should be wasted, so soak bread in it, or some cooked rice, or cabbage cooked above the grill. (Recipes later on.)

If the steak is a little tough (the butcher must warn you, but you can recognize it by the coarse fibre of the lean) sprinkle lemon juice over it, a teaspoonful of sugar and some salt. Then begin beating it with the back of a wooden spoon—both sides—on the chopping board to break down the fibres. In this way it is made tender enough to grill. As before.

FRIED STEAK

Any steak which is tender enough to grill will remain just as tender if it is fried. Snip off the surrounding fat and let it melt in an open pan or plate over moderate heat. When enough has melted and the bits are becoming crisply brown, put in the lean steak. Turn it over in a minute to sear the other side, and let it fry until slightly brown. Keep turning it.

BRAISED STEAK

When the steak is really tough, nothing will soften it except stewing. First fry it on either side for one minute in its own melted fat or in margarine in an open saucepan.

Also put into the saucepan some peeled, uncooked root vegetables; carrots, parsnips, turnips—one of each—and an onion. Let them fry for a few minutes, then shake on salt and pepper. Put in a teacupful of stock or water and a good splash of red wine if possible, or tomato juice. Clamp the lid on. When it comes to the boil, turn the heat to a simmer and let it cook for an hour and a half. At any rate until the steak is yielding when a fork is turned in it. Look at it half way through the time to see that the moisture has not all evaporated. If so, add some more water, which must be boiling so that the heat isn't reduced.

Vary this dish, especially if you have made enough for two days, by putting in on the second day some dried herbs; a teaspoonful of thyme, or one leaf of sage, or perhaps two or three cloves and peppercorns, a shake of red pepper or a chilli.

KIDNEY AND MUSHROOMS

If the kidney is smothered in its own fat, put it under the grill (moderate heat) just as it is, on a plate which must be fireproof. Drain away the surplus fat and keep turning the kidney as it cooks. It should be tender in about fifteen minutes.

If the kidney is not encased in its fat, grilling will only harden it. So it must be softened by simmering first. Enclose it with a little water or stock (and possibly a sliced onion) in a saucepan, closely lidded. Bring it to the boil, then turn the heat low to let it simmer for twenty minutes or so. Test it with a fork to see when it is tender. Then brown it by putting it with the juices on the plate under the grill; or over the heat to fry a little.

Cook the mushrooms separately, and not in the fat from the kidney. The flavour of mushrooms cooked in butter, however small the amount, is well worth the extravagance.

In fact, nothing is extravagant if it adds to enjoyment. That is, almost nothing. Within reason.

A walnut size, or two, of butter is enough to cook about four ounces of mushrooms, sliced or not. Keep turning them over until they look dark. If you like, or if you have only spared a small nut of butter, put a lid on after that to soften them more. Put them with the kidney under the grill when it is cooked. Keep a few back for mushrooms-on-toast next day for a mid-morning snack.

Don't forget chopped parsley or chives on cooked meat dishes. This is where I score with my window-box. I have it always fresh, in its season.

MINCED MEAT CASSEROLE

I make a great fuss of a half pound of minced meat. (I don't mean mince-meat which is fruit). As the butchers don't mince the best and therefore tender cuts of meat, the mince has to be stewed. That is the long, slow, moist cooking done in a casserole dish. I use an ordinary saucepan. Over moderate heat the fat runs out of the meat and fries the lean bits. After which I chop into it a large onion, (sometimes a nip of garlic, too), adding slices of whatever root vegetables I may have—turnip, swede or beetroot and a handful of sultanas. A spot of Worcestershire sauce or a glass of sharp red wine takes away the too-sweet flavour of these fruits.

Sometimes I put in a small spoonful of mixed dried herbs; or celery seeds, a few fennel seeds, a bayleaf, a pinch of sweet basil, thyme or marjoram; also a spoonful of tomato purée, a small sliced apple and a teacupful of stock or water.

With a good stirabout when it comes to the boil, I clap the lid on the pan, turn the heat to a glimmer and return once every half hour to add a little water if need be, to keep it from burning and to turn it over. This keeps the flavour neat and keeps fluidity to a minimum. It would be unpleasant as a stew I think.

In an hour and a half or so, it is tender enough for anyone. Larger quantities take longer, I never understand why. I might learn if I were to cook for a party, but then, I wouldn't present mince.

LIVER AND BACON WITH ONIONS

Get the calves' liver. Don't be put off with bullock's liver, which can be hard and sinewy. This is all right to eat in company, diverted by conversation.

First cut the fat off the bacon, snipping it across the rind. Let it sizzle over moderate heat in the saucepan. Fry the lean bacon in it, then take it out and keep it hot under the grill with *gentle* heat. Slice an onion, straight into the saucepan. Put the lid on and leave it to cook, turning once or twice, until it becomes light yellow. Take away the lid, push the onions to one side; slide in the sliced liver. Keep turning it gently until it is just brown. It should be cooked in less than ten minutes. Stick a fork in to try, as overcooking will harden it like leather. Slide it all on to the hot plate with the crisp bacon under the grill.

Raw celery is refreshing to follow this, or a crisply fresh tomato, or an apple.

FRIED APPLE

Slice a crisp, sharp cooker with the skin on (to keep its shape) into the saucepan-fry-pan to cook with the liver, the sausage or any other savoury meat. It gives just that pleasant piquancy which "cuts the grease" from the palate.

Or, cut the apple into chip shapes and grill them with steak or kidney.

LEMON SPRINKLER

One can't keep buying fresh lemons for the sprinkling one needs, and they go mouldy so quickly once they are cut, so get a bottle of the juice with a sprinkler top. They are very cheap, and keep a longish time, as one needs very little for meat, fish, salads or even pancakes.

FRIED CHICKEN WITH PIMIENTO

Buy a portion (one limb or two) or half a poussin which is such a tender little thing.

Forgive yourself if you have to use margarine instead of butter for frying. Rub the portion all over with a clean linen cloth dipped in salt. Sieve some flour all over it to make a coating and prevent it sticking to the pan. Melt about two ounces of "butter" in the saucepan. Use a spoonful of olive oil if you like. When it is hot, turn the heat to moderate and fry the chicken pieces, turning them occasionally with the egg slice.

If the heat is high the food sticks to the frying pan.

While it is frying, slice a pimiento (sweet red pepper); discard the seeds and fry the slices with the chicken. The flavour, imparting itself to the chicken, makes it more delicious still.

FRIED RABBIT WITH AUBERGINE AND PRUNES

Thank goodness one can also buy portions of rabbit nowadays. I could never eat a whole one. After the second day it gets left on the shelf.

It needs a little onion I always think. So I slice one into the dripping I fry the rabbit in (after wiping it clean like the chicken, and rolling it in flour—soya preferably—well salted). After ten or fifteen minutes of gentle frying the rabbit should be tender, but keep on until it is. Test it with a fork which should turn easily in the flesh when it is cooked. Just before that, slice an aubergine slant-wise and fry it with the rabbit. Sprinkle a little lemon on it at the last, and put it on a hot plate with plenty of chopped chives, parsley or watercress.

P.S. It is surprising how pleasant an accompaniment is a soaked prune or apricot, fried with the rabbit.

RICE, PLAIN

Usually I cook enough rice for two days. That is, a teacupful. Measure this into the saucepan. Let the cold tap rush on to it to send the dust to the top. Pour this off and repeat several times until the rice is clean and well drained. Add to it two measures (teacupfuls) of cold water. Add a teaspoonful of salt. Stir, and set it over moderate heat with the lid on. A transparent one if possible to see when it comes to the boil. When it does, turn the heat to *very* low. Don't take the lid off or touch the rice. Just leave it for twenty minutes. By that time all the water will be absorbed, the rice cooked soft and the grains well separated.

Get this operation under way before the grilling, etc., is started so that all will be ready at the same time.

Keep what you don't eat of the rice *uncovered* or it will go sour.

Reheat it next day or the day after, by pouring a little water over the dried top. Put on the lid of the saucepan and let it steam over gentle heat. In a few minutes, turn the whole lot upside down with the fish slice, and let it continue steaming. Don't let the bottom burn, as it will if the heat is high. (*See* Rice and Savoury Tomato, p. 49.)

FRIED RICE

Once the rice is softened it can be fried—again gently—in a little dripping or margarine. Keep turning it over so that it doesn't stick. In fact I put it around the meat I am grilling so that it becomes saturated with the escaping juices. Thereby all flavours are conserved. When I do this I don't fry bread or grill it with the meat. Enough starch is enough, I say.

RICE PUDDING

Rice pudding takes hours, which I rather like. I can potter in and out with good reason. But I make it quickly when I have some cooked plain rice from the previous day. I stir into the saucepan of cooked rice about one third of a tin of sweetened full-cream condensed milk, with half a teacupful of water. Stirring it well, and putting the lid on, it can be left over gentle heat until the milk is absorbed.

Make a nourishing dish of it by beating up an egg on to the fireproof dish, then mixing in the warmed, sweetened, milky rice. Leave it on the hob for a few minutes to heat, then under the grill to get a golden-brown top. I like a shake of nutmeg over this and a knob of butter to soak in, hot. But others may not like nutmeg.

Try a spoonful of apple or bramble jelly with it instead.

NOODLES WITH CHEESE

This is an easy and economical dish which I inevitably make when I have let some cheddar cheese go hard.

One handful of noodles is enough. Cover them in the saucepan with cold water. Put in a teaspoonful of salt, and bring all to the boil with the lid off. Let it boil fast for ten minutes or so, when the noodles should be really soft.

Grate a few ounces of cheese while they are boiling. Lift them out with a fork and the egg-slice and put them on a buttered grilling-plate. Shake the cheese over the noodles; add a knob of margarine and let it brown under the grill.

If there are any colourful things at hand, like fresh or tinned tomatoes, pimientos or gherkins, slice them and put them around the dish under the grill. Chop lots of parsley or nasturtium leaves to shake over, making a ring around the plate. This delights my eye which must always be appeased before I can eat with enjoyment.

NOODLES WITH MEAT AND MUSHROOMS

Once the noodles are cooked (keep the water in which they were boiled for soup), they can be dressed with a number of savoury things. Keep them simmering while the meat, etc., is being prepared.

Cut up and fry some mushrooms in a knob of butter on a fireproof plate. Slice some cooked, tinned meat, or liver sausage and put it in with the cooked mushrooms. When all have become hot right through, push them to one side; lift out the noodles on to the hot plate and pile over them the meat and mushrooms.

HOT PLATES

Always remember that a good meal can be utterly ruined if put on to a stone-cold plate. So if you use a china plate, make it hot under a moderate grill or stand it in hot water.

POTATOES

BOILED. My rule is always to boil them in their jackets. Boil enough for two or three days, and spread them out to dry. Like other starchy and glutinous foods they will go sour if left around in a damp condition.

Twenty minutes of fast boiling is enough in a cupful of water for the *new* ones.

Forty minutes, starting from cold water, will be needed at least for *old* ones. Stick a knife through to test when they are done. They should be simmered only, once they have been brought to the boil.

Skin them while they are hot—those you want to eat at once—by holding each on a fork. The skin pulls away easily with a sharp pointed knife with which the eyes can be turned out.

MASHED. Mash boiled potatoes *over moderate heat* (not when they're cold) with a lump of margarine, salt and pepper and a splash of milk. Use a fork, and when the mash is smooth, put it on the grilling-plate with the meat. Leave it under the grill for some minutes to become brown if you like it that way. You might spread grated cheese over it, roughening the top with a fork to give it that pleasant, uneven crisp effect, known as *gratinée*.

Mix a fresh egg with the potato as you mash it, using less milk in that case to soften it, to make it really creamy and nourishing.

SAUTÉ. Skin the boiled potatoes and slice them into a frying-pan or plate containing hot dripping or butter.

Keep turning them over until they are hot right through, or even until they become brown if you prefer. In either case, do mix in some finely chopped green thing—watercress, or mustard and cress—even a teaspoonful brightens the whole aspect.

GRILLED. Put sliced boiled potatoes on a buttered fireproof dish and leave them under the grill to become brown, turning them once.

CHIPS. Cut the boiled potatoes into chip shapes and grill them as described above. Uncooked potatoes are done in the same way, only they take longer—up to half an hour—and they must be turned occasionally. This is my way of cooking chips in my limited space, the atomsphere of which becomes overwhelming if I fry in deep fat, which is the conventional way of chip making.

The potatoes may be grilled *without fat*, which is a good thing to know if one is on a diet of austerity.

ROOT VEGETABLES

After peeling these, cut them up into small pieces. They are cooked more quickly so, in a cupful of boiling water. As they may take as long as twenty minutes to soften, you may need to add a little more water as it evaporates. Lift them out of their cooking water and put them in the juice of the meat around it, under the grill.

SWEDE MASHED WITH BACON

If I've grilled some bacon, nothing suits it so well (I

think) as cooked swede, mashed in the bacon fat with a nut of vegetable extract.

BUTTERED ONION

When I have some white fish, I like to eat with it, or separately, a dish of boiled onion, which I chop finely before cooking it. I like to drain it, mix it with a little pepper, salt and butter and keep it hot under the grill around the fish, with a grating of cheese on top.

CHICORY AND SEAKALE IN LEMON BUTTER

These white stalk vegetables I sometimes like to have with white fish, or just by themselves, like *asparagus*. After cooking them soft in the minimum of water, I put them on a hot grilling plate, with a lump of butter, some pepper, salt and a spoonful of lemon juice. I put it over the heat or under the grill for just the amount of time it takes to melt the butter.

SWEET CORN

All I ask to dip this into, when I eat it from the cone, is seasoned butter, very hot, on a hot dish. The cone is simmered in the minimum of water and it may take fifteen minutes or so to soften.

RUSSIAN SALAD

Any of the cooked root vegetables will do for assembling a Russian salad. Cut them into dice; find some cooked peas—tinned, or the frozen ones thawed, are excellent—and chop up a small onion, possibly also a clove of garlic. Take a forkful of mayonnaise and mix all together and rub a leaf of dried mint over it. Sometimes I like it hot, sometimes stone cold.

CHOPPING ONIONS

There is rarely any necessity to handle food. The deft manipulation of a knife, fork and spoon can avert such transference of flavours. The onion, for instance, need not intrude. Cut away the root. Stick a fork into where you cut. Cut away the tail (growing) end. Slit the brown skin downwards in three places with the point of the knife and strip it away. Holding the onion firmly on the fork, slash it criss-cross with the knife; then slice across the criss-crosses and watch the chopped onion falling into the salad or the cooking pot.

GREEN VEGETABLES

All the green vegetables must be cooked in a small cupful of boiling water. If they are first shredded finely—with a sharp, stainless, serrated knife on a chopping board—they will become tenderly cooked in ten minutes. Keep the lid on the saucepan, and turn them over once to give them oxygen and to see they are not burning at the bottom of the pan. Peas need more water and take twenty minutes.

In order that their fresh green look doesn't fade by sad delay, cook them at the very last, just when they are to be eaten. If something is grilling at the same time, lift them clear of their cooking water, let them drain before putting them alongside the meat, the juices from which will be ample sauce or "gravy". I like a little butter on them as well, with a shake of salt and black pepper.

CREAMED SPINACH

Some may think it a bother, but I like making a purée of the spinach. After cooking it quite tender, I rub it through a sieve with a wooden spoon, add salt and pepper, and a spoonful of cream or evaporated milk. Then I reheat it on my fireproof plate, turning it over and over until it is very hot all through. This is essential as it cools quickly, as cabbage does. The velvety texture of creamed spinach is unforgettable. I like it with a thick steak or with the wing of a chicken, hot.

BRUSSELS SPROUTS

As so much water is held within these minute cabbages if they are cooked and eaten whole, I prefer to shred them, or at least quarter them before cooking. They become cooked more quickly therefore and remain greener than when they are whole. I like them mixed with a nut of meat or vegetable extract and a lump of margarine, and possibly the inside of a fresh tomato.

Sometimes I rub them through a sieve, like the spinach, and mix them with cream.

Sometimes I cover them, after mixing them with a knob of butter, with a masking cheese sauce and brown it under the grill. This makes a satisfactory little meal with some chipolata sausages, pricked and grilled, whole.

VEGETABLE CUP

This sounds very grand and mysterious. It's my health-soup-cocktail. I pour all the juices from my cooked vegetables into my soup cup and drink it at once, before I begin my meal. It is full of mineral salts and of such good flavour. Yes, I take care of myself rather well.

TOMATO JELLY

This is refreshing, simple, and looks attractive set on some pale green, fringe-like leaves of endive.

A level teaspoonful of powdered gelatine is left in a round mould or cup to swell. After five minutes the cup is stood in a bowl of hot water to let the gelatine dissolve. A teaspoonful of spiced or garlic vinegar and another tablespoonful of water is added (hot if possible) and stirred. When the gelatine is quite dissolved, two tablespoonfuls of tomato purée and a teaspoonful of orange squash are stirred in and it is left to set in a cold place.

Make it more savoury when you choose by mixing in a

few shreds of onion and a pinch of powdered clove or cayenne pepper.

When it has set firmly—in a few hours maybe—stand the cup in hot water for a moment to release the jelly, and invert it on a plate before lifting off the cup.

ASPIC JELLY

By using more vinegar or lemon juice with the gelatine instead of water, a sharper, aspic jelly is made, with or without the tomato purée. When it is just beginning to set, drop into it here and there a few cooked peas, a spoonful of any diced cooked vegetable and chopped parsley. This makes the jelly colourful enough, but, it also encourages one to try setting other oddments in it, such as sliced hard-boiled egg, prawns, strips of cucumber or ham. Ring it around on a plate with crisp watercress or some finely shredded raw brussels sprouts dressed with mayonnaise.

TOMATO PURÉE

There are many ways of using up a tin of tomato purée, and it should be used within a week once it is opened, even though it is, as it should be, poured into a glass jar and closed with a non-corrosive lid, as with all acid foods.

Use it to make into tomato savoury ketchup.

Dilute it with a little water, and add a spot of Worcestershire sauce to make a tomato juice cocktail. This should be very cold.

Dilute it with vegetable juices and flavour it with onion to make a savoury jelly.

A spoonful or two added to a meat casserole gives it excellent flavour and good colour.

Any vegetable or meat stock, thickened with flour or not, can be made into a rich tomato soup by putting in a half cupful of tomato purée and letting it come to the boil to sterilize it. Add any milk or cream to this only to cool it. If the milk is boiled with tomato it will curdle.

TOMATO PASTE

This is a very concentrated form of purée so should be used with discretion and diluted quite a lot. It is so good, so economical, so compact and easy to store that I buy it when I can get it—the smallest tins possible, as they last so well.

SAVOURY TOMATO KETCHUP

This is one of my favourite dressings over a dish of rice, spaghetti or noodles, all the year round. I can use tomato purée from a tin when the tomatoes are out of season, and, as the year revolves, I use the different kinds of onion which are available—spring onions, shallots, the matured winter onions, leeks and garlic. (*See* Rice, p. 39 *and* Noodles, p. 40.)

A peeled section of GARLIC is squashed with the back of a spoon on the cooking plate. The tomato purée is added with a shake of powdered clove or ginger, pepper and salt, and made hot over the heat. And that is all.

The white top of the LEEK must be very finely shredded and simmered for a minute or two with the tomato, with a few ground black peppers and maybe a few fennel seeds with salt to flavour it.

The SPRING ONIONS are better uncooked, as the green stalks harden with cooking. So they should be chopped and added to the hot tomato.

The flavour of the ONION is altered and deepened if it is fried slightly in a knob of margarine or a little olive oil before the tomato is added. Sometimes I chop a piece of apple into it as well, and stir in a dozen or more sultanas, a pinch of thyme, red pepper and a bayleaf.

I always like the dish of rice surrounded by a ring of watercress or showered with chopped parsley.

VINEGAR

To prevent the vinegar becoming fertile—(the slippery little mothery plant that grows in it)—I boil it to *sterilize it.*

SPICED. I boil a teaspoonful of mixed spice in a pint of vinegar for five minutes, and bottle it when it is cold, corking it tightly. Boil without lid on pan.

GARLIC. Any part of a garlic section I have left over—and they vary in size so that I don't always want a whole one—I put it into a bottle of sterilized vinegar and keep it also corked.

CAPERS. Just when the petals have fallen off my nasturtium flowers I put the seeds into a little bottle of spiced vinegar. This transforms them to pickled "capers" (a good imitation) in a week.

PICKLED ONION. Any portion of onion I don't use is put into a little jar to become pickled in a week or less.

PICKLED CUCUMBER. Any chunks of cucumber can go in too. Vinegar is a good preservative.

PICKLED BEETROOT. This must be pickled separately as it turns the vinegar a rich red. It keeps well in the more mildly flavoured juice from a tin of sweet-sour gherkins.

RE-USING VINEGAR. All these things dilute the vinegar so that it loses its power to preserve. So I boil it with the lid off to reduce the water content before using it a second time.

Here I came to a full stop. Not that my friend would stop her happy pottering, but it was all she had written out—or rather, all that I could decipher. But I tried all her recipes to make sure I had transcribed them accurately. So far, I found them good.

VI

THE GRASS WIDOWER

"At last I can cook it the way I like it," he said. She, his fascinating, very young wife had gone home to mother for her annual stay. No glancing shafts of wit or suggestion had yet scratched the surface of her self-confidence in her own brand of "fancy" cooking, which flouted so many of the basic rules. He hated to discourage her, but he recalled often the meals his dear mother had cooked—salt, butter, pepper, no more. He would now do the same.

He wasn't very successful at first. He always seemed to be hungry. "What she calls my waste-line will soon waste away altogether", he told himself, half in hope, half in fear. One maxim was born of his initial ineptitude—"Store or you starve." So he bought a lot of tinned foods, fruits, sweetcorn on the cob, green beans and peas, soups, ham, tongue, cream and jams.

These were all very well, but nothing that came out of them matched his enjoyment of a thick *fillet steak*, lightly grilled either side, so that the blood ran out of it as it was cut. But fillet steak was too infrequent a find. His next discovery of very simply cooked food was fish, and this he grew to depend on a good deal, with a great deal of pleasure. I will set out as nearly as possible the ways he cooked it.

PLAICE, FILLETED (POACHED OR STEAMED)

A lump of butter (or margarine) is spread on a deep soup plate. The fillets of plaice lightly salted are put over that, skinny side up. Another plate covers that, and the "sandwich" is set over a saucepan containing boiling water. In ten or fifteen minutes (depending on the thickness of the fillets) the plaice should be cooked. The prong of a fork inserted near the skin is the test to see if it is yielding. Too much cooking will bring all the white opaque substance out of the fish and reduce the flavour. It will, of course, flow into the buttery juice on the plate, which is used for eating from, and a piece of soft bread will absorb everything without waste.

DOVER SOLE, POACHED IN BUTTER

This is cooked exactly in the same way as the plaice, when it is filleted. If it should be a cutlet—a chunk cut across the bone—or whole, it may take as long as twenty minutes to soften. The fork in this case is inserted near the bone to test if it is done. The flesh should come away from the bone easily. Because of the rich *calcium* content of bones, it is more nourishing to eat fish cooked with the bones in.

HALIBUT, STEAMED OR FRIED

STEAMED. Halibut is so thick usually, even when one asks that the cutlets should be cut thin, that it will take sometimes as long as twenty minutes to soften right through by steaming. It is always best to test it beforehand, however, in case it should overcook.

FRIED. As *white fish* contains no oil (it is all in the liver), some richness may be given to it, without destroying the sea flavour, by frying it in margarine after dipping it in flour. When the melted margarine is hot in the frying pan (the glass fireproof ones are nice to eat from), the cutlet is put in. A plate or a lid over the top keeps the heat consistent and cooks the fish right through, but the consequent moisture will prevent it from becoming brown. To achieve this the lid must be removed. When the moisture evaporates the underneath will become brown, so the fish should be turned once to let the other side become brown too. It is delicious cold, but must be skinned while hot.

WHITING

A cutlet from the larger fish is so much easier to manipulate than the whole of a smaller fish such as whiting, which, though it is cooked in half the time, takes twice the time to eat—picking one's way through the tiny bones —so tantalizing when one is hungry. The flavour is rather insipid, but if deft hands with a sharp knife have filleted these little fish, they can be given flavour and extra nutriment by dipping them in egg—beaten up on a plate with a flexible knife—then in wholemeal flour or fine breadcrumbs, before frying them gently in margarine.

TROUT

This small fish is so flavourful one might consider it well worth the bother of fussing with small bones. As it is a freshwater fish, it must be *absolutely fresh* and washed in salted water. The belly should be slit and cut along with scissors and the guts pulled out, but the head is left on for cooking. Turned over on a hot, buttered fireproof plate, it will be grilled in about ten minutes—five or more minutes either side. A squeeze of lemon juice over it seems to accentuate its particular flavour.

SKATE

This richly glutinous fish is so satisfying, and, because it is boneless, nothing need interrupt its transference from the plate to its predestined abode. Only the fin of skate is eaten (the body is so small) and what may be called the bones are flexible, thick, and non-spiky so that the flesh is easily separated from them. A cutlet of any dimension can be chosen to satisfy the birdlike or wolfish appetite.

Dipped in salted flour (or egg and breadcrumbs) it is best fried in dripping or margarine over moderate heat, with occasional turnings to let every side cook evenly and thoroughly. Since they are thinner, two cutlets are more quickly cooked than one large one. If they are about an inch and a half thick they should be cooked in about twenty minutes.

A plate will be made hot ready for use if put over the frying-pan, but should not be put over until the fish is well browned. This closure of the pan will, of course, create moisture, so the plate should be taken off quickly with the moisture clinging to it, and then drained.

RED MULLET

These are little and good, with the flavour of fresh lobster. The fins are cut off, when the fish are washed and beheaded, and they are cooked with the guts in. Grilled on a buttered plate—a few minutes either side, with a little salt and cayenne pepper added—they can be savoured as a delicacy, even if inadequate for a meal.

FRESH SALMON CUTLET

COLD. Steam the cutlet between plates over boiling water, BUT, if it is to be eaten cold, do not put butter on it as butter (or any solid fat) separates itself and hardens as it cools. A dessertspoonful or less of olive oil, which mingles and congeals with the fish, is best, with a few drops of lemon juice (or white vinegar) and some pepper and salt. Turn the cutlet(s) over in this and leave to *marinate* (soak) for a little while—even an hour or more. The steaming should not go on for more than ten minutes before testing. On no account should the salmon be overcooked.

Take the top plate off as soon as it is cooked so that condensed steam will not drip into the salmon as it cools. Skin it before it cools.

HOT. As salmon is an oily fish, that fact must be taken into account if one is on a diet. It may be steamed (poached) in lemon juice only, a little milk—or even water—just enough to moisten it. The fish will release its own juices once it begins to get hot.

FRIED. Fry it in the same way as the halibut was fried, and it should then be eaten hot.

HERRING

GRILLED. Equal with salmon for richness is the herring. The strength of its flavour, however, the subsequent deodorizing and washing up; the intricate pattern of bones; its capacity for multitudinous breeding (and consequent cheapness) have put the herring in a low class—almost one of the Untouchables—with the finicky. But the fastidious palate rejoices in its unashamed individuality and self-assertion.

CLEANING. It needs a little care in the cleaning. First the scales, which are firmly fixed to the skin when the herring is fresh, must be scraped off. If the fish is held on a flat board and its tail gripped, a knife held upright and stroked towards the head will bring the scales away. After a rinse under the cold tap, the head must then be tackled. It should be cut just through the bone, then held tightly, and with a quick twist it will come away, dragging with it most of the guts. A sharp knife or, better, the scissors must then be inserted in the belly to cut down towards the tail, taking care not to split the *roes*, which are pulled out and put on a separate plate until they are about to be cooked. The body must now be washed again under the cold tap, when the inedible remaining guts—the silver and the black—can be pushed out with the back of the thumb-nail.

After that (the grill may be getting hot meanwhile) the herring is put on the grilling-plate under the red-hot grill and in five or more minutes it should be softened on the one side. Five or more minutes on the reverse side, and the herring is ready to eat, with salt, pepper, and perhaps a little lemon juice.

FRIED. Herring can, of course, be fried also, in the same was as the halibut was fried. The traditional way in the North is to roll the herring in medium oatmeal; put it into a hot frying-pan with a nut of dripping, and cook it without a lid, turning it over occasionally, with loving care, at a *moderate* heat.

THE ROES. These are rolled in flour, and that makes it easy to pull away any slippery, stringy bits, which are discarded. The roes are then ready to be fried *gently* in any kind of dripping or fat. There will be the hard, eggy, female roes and the soft, paste-like, male ones. A high heat will make them spit, and overcooking will harden them abominably. Roes may be kept for a separate snack, on toast, or fried with tomatoes and sauté potatoes. Alternatively they may be baked (covered with butter paper until the last few minutes), or fried, with the body of the herring.

MACKEREL, GRILLED

Tradition has decreed that the mackerel (oily too, but less so than the herring) should be cut across the flesh as deeply as the bone, but not through it, in three or four places, before grilling. It is a harder fish than the herring, and one makes quite a filling meal with brown, buttered bread, and whatever fresh, raw, green things may be at hand, or celery.

LOBSTER WITH SALAD

He, our Grass Widower, found the cooking of vegetables too complicated, and he had not mastered the timing technique before his grass widowerhood drew to its close.

"Why bother?" he said, crunching a sweet, fresh, raw carrot. "It only spoils the flavour, and I still have my molars. . . . The Time Factor? . . . yes, but I crunch while I grill. Keeps me in strength and sharpens my appetite while the aroma of my fish or meat is pervading the house."

But when he arrived home with a fresh lobster, cleverly cloven lengthwise, ready to be pulled from its soft shell and eaten, he sometimes preferred to set the pulled flesh aside on a plate while he prepared a simple salad.

RAW VEGETABLE SALAD

Usually it was just the heart of a lettuce (he could never be bothered to de-grit the outer, coarse leaves) pulled apart and turned over on a plate with a sprinkling of olive oil, lemon juice, white pepper and salt.

It might be the heart of a celery, simply dipped in salt.

Occasionally he grated a CARROT (finely), a TURNIP (coarsely), or shredded a piece of WHITE-HEART CABBAGE very finely, like cotton, and a small sliced ONION. He found that a firm, white-heart cabbage would serve for salad portions for a week. Only the dried outer surface of the cut portion had to be shaved off and discarded. The rest was juicy and firm until the very end. He even liked it, raw as it was, shredded with a TOMATO, to eat with his fillet steak or grilled chop.

CRAB

Patience deserted him entirely when he tried to deal with this crustacean. Eating privately, and for enjoyment, with no conversational obligations, he set about satisfying his hunger quite methodically. First he turned on the radio to the most cheerful programme he could find advertised; then he rolled up his sleeves; collected a large tray, the nut-crackers, a bone crochet hook, a fork, a cellar of salt, a heart of celery standing in a glass, some brown bread and butter and a vast table napkin.

Pulling away the grey matter (he called it the fronds) in a clump at the centre, and discarding it, he could eat freely of all that remained—the flaky flesh, the soft yellow, flavourful substance in the body—intermittently with the cracking of the claws and the hooking out of their pinky, succulent flesh.

CRAYFISH, PRAWNS AND SHRIMPS

These soft crustaceans require a less robust operation. No implement is needed to pull off the heads, the tails, the legs and the shells. It *can* be done with the fingers, but, though more tedious, may be done with a knife and fork. Shrimps take ages, and for that reason he sometimes bought them ready-peeled, knowing, but deliberately forgetting, that they had been peeled by someone else's hands.

The CRAYFISH being of such a sweet and delicately delicious flavour, he ate them as he bought them, freshly boiled in water.

But the PRAWNS and the SHRIMPS he liked occasionally to fry gently in a knob of butter. A few minutes only, adding a little salt and red pepper.

PARSLEY BUTTER

Once he fried some finely chopped parsley in the butter with the prawns, and enjoyed it so much. He tried the same idea with *watercress* and even preferred it.

He liked to eat crisp-bread, with a scrape of butter on it with these little fish. "Keeps my weight down", he told himself as he bought the wax-paper-wrapped packet, and, as he said that, he realized that he hadn't starved after all. In fact, he had done himself rather well.

WASHING UP

If there had been one serious deterrent, it had been the

washing up. But on the second day of his temporary living and cooking alone, he had been given a tip—about the cold water wash up. He was so delighted to find how rapidly the sticky gluten of fish, bread and other things softened in cold water, that his distaste for washing up was replaced by interest.

He evolved the simple technique of pushing off the remnants from the plates with paper on to paper; rolling it up for the bin. Under the cold-water tap he mopped any dishes he had used, let them stand, filled with water, for a few minutes while he cleared the table and put on the kettle to boil. By that time the most hardened gluten was easy to remove with a rub of a woven nylon pad. In a bowl he set the dirty things, with a spot of detergent, pouring hot water in to dissolve the grease. A wag of the mop and a final rinse under the tap left the dishes scrupulously clean. As he had a plate rack, the dishes were stood upright to drip, and no cloth was ever used for wiping.

Sometimes a harder rub on a saucepan was necessary, to loosen anything stuck fast. For this he again used the little nylon pad, which didn't hurt his fingers or set his temper on edge.

BURNISHING ALUMINIUM

To bleach an aluminium saucepan which went black because he boiled water in it, he boiled more water in it with a saltspoonful of tartaric acid (though apple skins or rhubarb would have done). The outside he burnished with a little pad of soapy steel wool (he squeezed some out of his tube of shaving soap)—a gentle circular rub and a rinse. The result was startlingly bright.

Even more brightly gleamed the pans which were CHROMIUM plated, the surface of which must never be touched even with the smoothest abrasive. Water and a soft cloth were the most successful polishes he found.

THE SILVER

The most sobering thought, however, was the tarnished silver. He could not let it remain so to mar his dear wife's pleasure at her home-coming. There was only one day to go, when, confessing his dilemma to a friend, he learned the most simple tip of all. He bought a roll of aluminium foil, tore off a small strip and put it in his sink, with a handful of washing soda. When the kettle was boiling he poured the water over the soda and the aluminium. Then, taking each silver article (gripped with the tongs) he immersed it in the water, seeing that the article touched the aluminium foil. The tarnish disappeared instantly.

When he had untarnished everything he could lay his hands on (this kind of magic gave him pleasure), he put the silver articles in a basin of warm water and lifted them out to dry. When they had dripped dry, he rubbed them with a soft, clean cloth, and put them away.

And, as he sat before his fire, with his dressing-gown keeping his knees warm, and his slippers on his feet, he sipped a comforting glass of old port, recalling the details of his wife's departure and anticipating the details of her return.

He visualized the surprise in her eyes when he brought before her the repast he had prepared—cold fresh salmon with sliced cucumber (it was there, standing with its end in cold water, ready to slice), lettuce hearts which he had washed and hung up in a linen cloth to drip and keep crisp, and the BRANDY PEACHES which he had invented himself. The peaches he had bought fresh, peeled and sliced them, scooped them into a screw-top jar, shaken caster sugar over them, and poured a wineglassful of brandy over them, closing the top tightly so that they would be well soaked with all the bouquet held captive.

She *would* be delighted!

VII

THE CAREER WOMAN

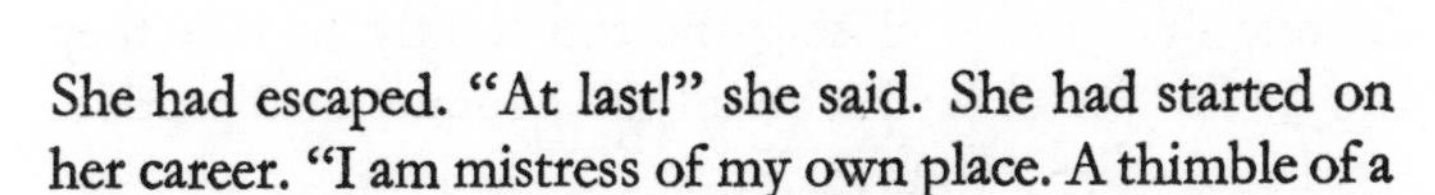

She had escaped. "At last!" she said. She had started on her career. "I am mistress of my own place. A thimble of a place, but here I can have my own way."

However, the proportions were good, and already her deft hands and measuring eye had created a transforming touch here and there, so that Satisfaction seemed to rest in her for lengthening periods.

"And I shall cook, after my fashion", she reflected, "whatever the result."

She thought of the Tyrant—who had come as a nurse-cum-governess, and who had remained to be house-keeper-cum-cook—and the staple diet she had imposed—boiled beef, boiled puddings, boiled coffee. Efficient, formidable and "touchy", the Tyrant had kept her out of the kitchen. Curious to think now of the escape route—the years of study, diligence masking rebellion—and now, a salary, independence, and a kitchen *of her own.*

Because her time in it was limited by that very Career which gave her the freedom of her kitchen, she had to cook many things in advance. Although she had no refrigerator

—yet—she found that a piece of meat large enough to last for days, once it was cooked, would keep in good condition in a little wire-netted food cage set near the open window on the stone slab she had procured from a stone mason.

As she didn't always want to use her oven, she developed a successful technique of POT-ROASTING her meat. She began simply, and developed more aromatic themes when she had talked cooking with her friends.

ROAST BEEF

In a saucepan over moderate heat she put in her joint of beef—topside when she could get it—fatty side down, and put the lid on. This confined the smell and therefore the flavour while the fat melted. But it also confined the moisture which dropped down over the beef. Thus was introduced the principle of *wet cooking*. This is opposed to *dry cooking* (in an oven or under a grill) whereby the moisture evaporates and the time needed for cooking is much less. Once the meat is made wet, however, the cooking time is considerably extended.

This joint, weighing about two pounds, would roast by dry cooking in an oven in about an hour and a quarter. Roasting in a pot with the lid on, gathering moisture, it would need about two hours to become tender. The coarser cuts take longer still. However, there was economy in heating as her oven took fifteen minutes or more to become hot, and the top heat could be turned to a simmer once the pot had become really hot.

Sometimes she put one or more whole, peeled onions in with the beef to give it extra flavour. Sometimes she liked the flavour neat, with just pepper and salt.

Eating what she needed from it while it was hot, she left the rest to become cold so that she could slice away at it the following evening when she arrived home, appeasing her hunger without delay.

ROAST VEAL

Although veal is pale and less full-bodied in flavour and nutriment than beef, she liked it because it was always so lean and so tender. She liked to give savour to it, and oil as well, so she fried it lightly all over in a tablespoonful of olive oil to seal in its juices. Then she put in a "bouquet garni"—a bunch of herbs—a leaf of sage, a bayleaf, a good pinch of thyme and a leaf of mint. Occasionally she put a small glass of red wine in with it, giving it colour and sharpening the flavour slightly.

With the lid tightly fitted and the heat kept moderate, the veal—again about two pounds—became pot-roasted in about an hour because of its young tenderness.

ROAST LAMB

The lamb, also a youngster, is so tender, it will roast quickly. But, unlike veal, the younger it is the fatter it is. So that the joint of lamb should be put in the roasting pot at a low heat with the lid on to allow its fat to melt. After that the meat should be turned over occasionally to allow the lean to become saturated with the fats and whatever herbs, spices or vegetables have been put in the pot with it.

At the closure of the day, the woman with a Career may feel that she can safely put garlic in her pot-roast—rubbing it over the lamb or sticking in a clove of it between the fat and the lean. If she were going out for the evening, after her garlic feast, she took care to eat a piece of parsley which dispelled the savour and she could meet the world full face.

BROWNING OFF THE POT-ROAST

Since it is the hot, melted fat which gives the brown crispness to the outside of the meat, whereas the moisture keeps it soft, this must be evaporated to regain the conditions whereby the meat can be browned off. Simply by taking the lid off the saucepan and letting it remain over the heat after the meat has become tenderly cooked, the water will evaporate, and the meat will become brown underneath in the fat. It should be turned to allow the other side to become brown, too, possibly on the following night when the meat may be re-heated for the second hot meal from the same joint.

ROAST PORK

When she bought a piece of pork, she treated it with great respect and it brought its own reward. Her own knives always seemed clumsy tools compared with those of the butcher, who slit the skin in narrow strips, then across, making diamond-shaped sections of what would become the crackling. This way of criss-crossing the skin makes it a much more manageable bite than when it is left in long tape measures.

She rubbed olive oil and salt into the slit skin; rubbed over the whole piece a cut clove of garlic, and stuck a few leaves of sage here and there in it.

Slicing an onion she spread it over a shallow baking-pan with a spoonful of mayonnaise, a sprig of rosemary and a bayleaf. In this she turned the pork over a few times, then left it to marinate (soak) in the juices for an hour or so.

She chose to use her oven to roast the pork at a very moderate heat—350° F. or Gas No. 6—for an hour or two, depending on the thickness of the piece. The skin must be uppermost if it is to become crisp and crunchy, so that the dry, oven roasting is most suitable to get this effect. This crackling remains crisp while the pork is hot. Next day, when the pork is cold, the crispness vanishes.

ROAST VEGETABLES

Ten minutes before she put the pork in to roast, while the oven heat was mounting, she put in on the roasting tin, peeled, halved potatoes—just enough for the first hot meal—and several peeled, whole onions.

ROAST POTATOES deteriorate after the first roasting. The crispness sags out of them and they harden if re-heated.

ROASTED ONIONS, however, may be re-heated with advantage as they first soften, then become more deeply flavoured as they brown off.

Carrots, parsnips, turnips, Jerusalem artichokes and swedes should be boiled soft before setting them around the meat in its juices to roast, about twenty minutes before it is due to come out of the oven.

BAKED POTATO

The larger the potato, the longer it takes to cook, of course. If it is a really large one, the cooking should be at a rather low heat so that it penetrates right through and the potato is cooked evenly inside and out.

After scrubbing it, it is put on the floor of the oven, outside the baking tin—when a cake or meat is being cooked, or even a rice pudding—anything which takes long to cook, not to waste the heat.

When the potato is cooked, there is nothing else to be done except cut it right through, hold it in a napkin in the hand and make a hole in the middle with a spoon; fill that up with butter and eat it with salt, comfortably before the fire.

HOT ROLLS

When she had no potatoes, or, perhaps from choice, she took bread with her meat instead. A thick slice, or a roll, was put into the oven during the last ten minutes of roasting the meat. It emerged like freshly baked, soft bread, crisp on the outside, even if it had been yesterday's or that of the day before.

BOILED CHICKEN

"What is the use of having a career", she said to herself one day, "if I can't give myself a treat now and again. I'll buy myself a chicken—a boiler to begin with, for practice, as they are cheaper."

So she bought as small a boiler as she could. It was plump and the flesh was white which assured her, as she had read, that it was in good condition.

CLEANING it was her first problem, so she read a book which described the process in detail and she did this. She cut away the trussing strings and let the cold water from the tap run through its de-gutted inside. Laying the chicken on a tray, she wiped it over, inside as well, with a non-fluffy linen cloth, then rubbed it all over with salt.

TRUSSING it again—tying the legs and the wings together, tucking them under the body and tying them to it—was a precaution she was warned to take. Once the heat gets at the limbs they shoot out and then stiffen beyond recall.

THE GIBLETS—the neck, heart, kidneys, liver and crop are what the poulterer calls the "edible offal"—are put in the pot with the chicken to be boiled, too. They must be washed under the cold-water tap, and any green or yellow bits cut off and thrown away.

Some flavouring herbs and an onion are almost essential to develop the delicate taste of the chicken. Not too much to overwhelm it. Perhaps a sprig of mint, and a teaspoonful of thyme or marjoram, with one section of garlic and an onion. Two or three cloves are good with it, too, and possibly a bayleaf as well, with a teaspoonful of salt and a shake of red pepper. No potatoes or rice should be put in with the chicken as they draw the flavour to themselves and so deprive the chicken. Besides, these starchy foods turn sour if left more than a day in a wet condition, whereas the chicken can be kept for several days without harm. Any of the root vegetables may be cooked with it, but if they are cooked for too long a time, they lose their flavour, and in this case, the chicken and the soup will benefit.

Even if only a pint of water is added in which to cook the chicken—and it must be simmered gently once it has been brought to the boil—much more liquid will come from the chicken itself, so that there will be quite a quantity of rich soup.

THE SOUP, as well as ample portions of the boiled chicken, will provide rich evening meals for the best part of a week for anyone living alone, returning home fatigued, ready and eager for immediate re-invigoration.

POT-ROAST CHICKEN

Having prepared the chicken (a roaster or a young boiler) in the way described, it can be pot-roasted in a few ounces of butter or dripping, over gentle heat at first until the juices are released from the chicken.

Half a teacupful of vegetable juices such as tomato or green vegetable stock may be put in with the same measure of cider or, preferably, white wine.

With the lid on the saucepan causing added moisture, the chicken will simmer without drying up, and should be tender in one to one and a half hours, depending on the age and the size of it. A fork twisted in the leg will show when it is ready as the flesh will break away easily.

That is the time to take the lid from the pan, to let the moisture evaporate, still over low heat. When it dries, the chicken will become brown underneath, providing a crisp surface from which to carve a portion for one, leaving the rest to be browned on successive occasions.

JELLIED CHICKEN

The next day, the juice from the chicken will have congealed, that is, if it has been cooked in the minimum of liquid and evaporated as described. So instant satisfaction awaits the Career Woman the moment she returns and is ready to eat, especially if she has brought home with her (or has stored) a packet or tin of potato crisps, and has some fresh, green vegetable, such as watercress, lettuce or endive, which need not be cooked.

CHICKEN CUTLET (FRICASSÉE)

By this idea she did not mean to imply the cutlet, so-called, which comprises a modicum of chicken mashed with quantities of potato and breadcrumbs, then baked.

She cut a robust slice of chicken from the breast, turned it over on a plate moistened with milk (a beaten egg was too much for one), rolled it in flour and fried it gently in a knob of butter on a fireproof plate. She liked to fry a piece of apple with it when she could, keeping back a piece from those she was stewing for a sweet course.

GRILLED CHICKEN

Several thick slices of the boiled chicken, with some of its savoury jelly put over and around, can be quite delicious re-heated by grilling. Turn once, and put strips of bread alongside to toast simultaneously, as well as a sliced pimiento which suits chicken admirably. The red, the yellow and the green ones are equally good, and make any dish of food attractive. They will keep a week without becoming over-ripe if they are bought in a rather firm condition.

RE-HEATING FOOD

Long grilling hardens food, so don't re-grill it. But food softened by steaming may be re-heated by grilling.

All food which is re-heated must be made hot right through under or over gentle heat, so that the outside is not hardened leaving the inside half cold. Gentle frying is almost the easiest way, but account must be taken of the extra fat needed and absorbed into the food.

If extra fat is not forbidden by necessity or choice, the palate may be freshened by a squeeze of lemon juice over the fried food just before eating it. Other piquancies to give the same effect are pickled gherkins, pickled beetroot, cranberry sauce, apples stewed without sugar, fresh, sliced tomatoes, sections of peeled grapefruit, sliced plums, squashed fresh redcurrants or sliced gooseberries, all made hot.

Some days the career would seem an arid business. At least the Career Woman would feel dried up, or filled up, with nothing much else but sandwiches, sandwiches all day long. So then the evening meal just had to be vegetables. Relaxing in her arm-chair with a self-indulgent glass of good sherry in her hand, she could think as she sipped, and soon she would gain Dutch courage to face the drudgery of peeling and washing the vegetables. The sliced roots went into the saucepan first, and when they were nearly done the shredded green things went on top, so that they were all ready together. A half-teaspoonful of meat or vegetable extract and a lump of butter gave them the extra nutriment and flavour which she liked.

SPAGHETTI AND CHEESE

When the meals during the day had not been so starchy—when salads and fruit had played their refreshing part in the diet—she might like to make herself a spaghetti dish. She preferred it a foot long, unbroken. In order that it should remain so, she held a bunch of it over a saucepan of boiling salted water, and, as the ends were immersed, they softened and curled around without snapping off. In fifteen minutes or so, depending on the thickness of the spaghetti, it was softly cooked and ready to lift out of the cooking water with a perforated egg-slice to drain it.

Twirled over a buttered fireproof dish, the dressing of grated or sliced cheese could now be put on and all grilled a golden brown.

Sometimes she grated orange peel to mingle with the cheese. Sometimes she boiled a chopped onion with the spaghetti, and a clove as well. Sometimes she covered it over with a cheese sauce which she made carefully, following these directions.

CHEESE SAUCE

A smallish saucepan will waste less, but a medium-sized one is easier to manipulate, even for a small amount. A *flat-ended* wooden spoon is a boon for mixing. The cheese must be grated ready, as everything happens quickly from now on. Ready-grated Parmesan cheese is most flavourful, and though less therefore is needed, it still is expensive. Good flavoured Cheddar or Cheshire is excellent if left to go hard before grating. Hang it up in a muslin cloth in a cold, airy place, or put it with its paper covering in a cardboard sugar carton in a refrigerator.

Melt a knob of margarine (the size of a large walnut) in the saucepan over moderate heat. Sift in, through the strainer, a heaped dessertspoonful of flour and let it sizzle. *Draw it away from the heat* and put in a spoonful of milk (hot or cold) and mix it all to a smooth paste. Add another spoonful of milk and mix again, keeping it absolutely smooth. Keep adding milk until the consistency is like moderately thin cream. Put the saucepan back over the heat and stir without stopping until it all comes to the boil, when it will thicken in half a moment. Again, draw it away from the heat, and that is the time, not before, when the grated cheese (an ounce or two) is to be stirred in. *Don't cook it*, or it will become stringy. Mix in half a teaspoonful each of salt, pepper and dry mustard, and scoop it over any cooked food—fish, cauliflower, mixed root vegetables, or rice, etc. The golden-brown hue it will assume under the grill will demand another rich colour to go with it, dark green or red things, watercress, chives, tomatoes, pimientos, shredded in no time with a serrated knife.

RAVIOLI

This consists of little mounds of minced meat enclosed between sheets of macaroni paste and stamped out into squares—about an inch. They have to be immersed in water and brought to the boil, then simmered *gently*, so that they don't disintegrate, until the macaroni is quite soft. This may take twenty minutes or so.

When the strips, or sheets of these little squares are lifted out of the saucepan, they should be put onto a very hot, buttered plate and, when possible, covered with a dressing of grated cheese, tomato ketchup, or perhaps butter and chopped watercress.

GNOCCHI

A simplified form of this savoury dish is made like this. Half a pint of milk and water is brought to the boil in a saucepan. A heaped tablespoonful of semolina with half a teaspoonful of salt is poured in, stirring all the time. When it begins to thicken, after five minutes of boiling, it is left to become cold and stiff. It is then easy to scoop out almond shapes with a large teaspoon, and set them on a buttered grilling-plate, leaving enough semolina to cover the plate for a similar dish on the following day. A cheese sauce is then poured over the "almonds", some grated cheese shaken over that and toasted under the grill until it is a golden brown. The underneath has to be made equally hot by setting it for a few minutes over moderate heat.

THE SWEET COURSE

Having conquered the difficulties about providing herself with a meat or a savoury course which she could eat almost at once, the Career Woman began to devise the methods whereby she could prepare her sweet course in advance also. She kept an emergency stock of tinned fruits as well as sealed jars of cream, and she kept a wicker basket of fresh fruits which she sometimes mingled with the tinned fruits to make a salad. In this case, as in many others, she made enough to last for two or more days.

FRUIT SALAD

Into a stone jar she emptied a small tin of fruit—plums, grapes or cherries. Skinning a grapefruit free of the coarse outer and fine inner skin as well, she put in the sections; also the sections of a peeled orange or tangerine, a peeled, quartered pear and a tablespoonful of demerara sugar. If the orange was thin skinned, she sliced it, skin and all to put in.

CITRUS SKINS

She found that the coarser type of orange skin was very juicy and easy to grate, which she did before peeling the fruit, storing the grated peel covered with castor sugar in a covered jam jar.

In a separate jar she stored the grated rind of lemons. In this simple way she had, ready for her use, rich flavouring for mixing into cakes, biscuits, jellies and even savoury dishes.

ORANGE DRINKS

Whatever was left from the portion of orange, as well as all the peel and the pips, she put into a jug with a tablespoonful of sugar, covered it with cold water and left it several days to mature. This she could pour off to drink, and keep filling up with more sugar and water, and the strength remained in it for a week.

FRUIT JELLY

Because she didn't care for synthetic flavours, she preferred to make jellies from natural fruit juices.

She made enough for two days, never for more, because jellies pick up bacteria and may therefore be unfit to eat after the second day. In fact, she usually made one at a time and left it overnight in a cold place to set, covered with cambric to keep the flies and the dust out but to let the air in to it.

Leaving a level teaspoonful of powdered gelatine to swell in a sundae glass with a dessertspoonful of cold fruit juice for five minutes, she then added a teacupful of the fruit juice, hot, and stirred it until the gelatine had quite dissolved, adding whatever sugar she pleased.

When the jelly had begun to set was the time to sink into it whatever slices or sections of fruit she had, so that they remained poised in it instead of sinking in a heap to the bottom.

LEMON, ORANGE AND GRAPEFRUIT JELLY

There was wisdom, she thought, in a suggestion that came from a friend, to keep a bottle of lemon squash, as well as the orange and the grapefruit squash with which to make jellies from these fruits. She diluted the juice slightly, added more sugar or mixed in any juices left from fruit salad or tinned fruits. At other times she might make the jelly into a "chiffon" (see the recipe for port wine chiffon jelly, p. 83) and set into it small pieces of sponge cake which softened and spread out in the jelly and made a fascinating sweet course, especially when there was some ice-cream to pile over it.

KEEPING ICE-CREAM FROZEN

It's all very well to buy a block of ice-cream on your way home, but it will soon melt in the atmosphere if there is no refrigerator. But, if it is wrapped in a good thickness of newspaper and then placed between two cushions and left in the shade, it will keep its shape for about three hours.

SEMOLINA PUDDING

This can be made in a wink over a high heat. Half a pint of milk and a level dessertspoonful of sugar is stirred as it comes to the boil in a saucepan. When it is frothily boiling up, a heaped dessertspoonful of semolina is sprinkled in, the stirring continued for a few more minutes while it all thickens, and it is ready to eat.

The difficulties about getting an extra bottle of milk are eliminated if a third of a tin of sweetened condensed milk is diluted with half a pint of water (no extra sugar is needed), stirred until it boils, when the semolina is poured in and cooked as before. These quantities are doubled when one is hungry, or if the first course contains no rice, bread or potato.

GLAZED PEAR

She bought small quantities of unripe pears at intervals, so that she usually had one that was just right. Pressing it gently near the stem to prove that it was soft and therefore ripe, she then peeled it, cut it in half and cut out the core. Setting the half pears flat side down she covered them with fine sugar and left them to absorb it before eating them with cream. She decided before much experience that there is no substitute for real cream with pears or apples. So what she saved in cost with these plentiful, common fruits, she expended in creamy luxury.

When she had some bramble jelly, or crab-apple jelly, she warmed a large spoonful and poured it over the pears, letting it set again to form a glaze.

CHOCOLATE PEAR

At another time she would melt a bar of milk chocolate in a cup over gentle heat, pour it over the halved, peeled pear and leave it to become cold, by which time the chocolate had set firmly again.

STEWED PEARS

For this simple sweet she used the hard cooking pears which never ripen. As they are rather tasteless they need sugar, perhaps a spoonful of jam, or some lemon juice and honey in the teacupful of water in which they must be simmered in a closed saucepan to soften them; or, possibly, a few fine slices of grapefruit or orange and some golden syrup. The excess moisture can be evaporated away once the pears are softened, by continuing to cook them with the lid off.

APPLE CRUMBLE

After stewing a sliced apple on a shallow dish with a spoonful of water and sugar (or with a spoonful of golden syrup without water) a pleasant crunchy effect is made by covering the top with breadcrumbs and demerara sugar. Before the underneath of the stewing-plate, or dish, becomes cold (re-heat it if it has), put it under the hot grill to let the sugar melt and the breadcrumbs become brown. They will be partly fruit-sugar soaked, partly crisp, sweet and yet sharp.

CHOCOLATE MOUSSE

This is a special treat and yet, made in this way is simple. The white is drained out of an egg into a mixing basin. The yolk with a two-ounce bar of chocolate is put into a dish over a bowl of hot water and whipped up with a fork as the chocolate melts.

Separately, the white of the egg is whisked to a very stiff froth, then spooned into the chocolate, stirred gently with the mixing fork, and left in a cold place to set. It is ready to eat as soon as it is quite cold.

PORT WINE CHIFFON JELLY

This must be mixed in a strong basin. A level teaspoon ful of crystal jelly is left to swell in a spoonful of *cold* water for five minutes. A spoonful of hot water is then added, and the basin stood over hot water until the gelatine is quite dissolved. About a level teaspoonful of fine sugar is stirred in, and finally a good-sized wineglassful of port wine. When the jelly begins to set (it sticks to the sides of the basin but is wobbly in the middle), that is the moment when it should be whisked to a stiff froth. It should be left to set in the coldest place possible.

When it is set firm it is ready to eat.

EVAPORATED MILK MOUSSE

However nice a jelly is, fresh cream over it makes it nicer. If there is no fresh cream, evaporated milk must come to the rescue.

In fact, a pleasant cream mousse or whipped cream can be made with evaporated milk, by adding a teacupful of it to a teaspoonful of dissolved, slightly sweetened gelatine, and whisked to a froth when it begins to congeal, just as the port wine chiffon jelly was made.

Any flavouring must be added before the whisking begins, such as a teaspoonful of COCOA, half that amount of COFFEE powder, or a few drops of VANILLA or ALMOND essence, to make that kind of cream mousse.

EVAPORATED MILK

The remains of a tin of unsweetened evaporated milk will keep fresh for a day or two if put into a jug and left open to the air, covered with muslin only, to keep the flies out; or, tightly screwed down in a glass jar in a refrigerator it will keep for several days. But these are the purposes for which it may be used so that, though living alone, one is not inhibited about opening a tin:

For making a cream mousse, or whipped cream with gelatine.

As cream in black coffee.

As cream over fruit, ice-cream or jelly. (Mix a little sugar with it as it is sometimes slightly salty.)

To dilute with water to make a cup of chocolate.

To mix with scrambled egg instead of milk.

To mix with cake dough instead of milk.

To mix with egg to make crême caramel.

To mix into mayonnaise as cream.

To mix with icing sugar to make a cake filling.

To mix with purée of spinach or brussels sprouts.

To mix with mashed potatoes instead of milk.

To add to a plate of hot soup as cream.

To mix with icing sugar and cocoa as a chocolate sauce.

For making cheese sauce or other masking sauce.

For making rich custard.

But it is *not* good with tea as a substitute for cream or milk. And it is useless to attempt to make a junket with it, though it makes a pleasant topping, once the junket is firmly clotted with fresh milk.

While she was round and about, or abroad, in pursuit of her career, she had acquired a fascinating collection of air-tight and colourful tins. "So I must make biscuits to keep in them," she said. "It will be so amusing to keep a different kind in each different tin, so that they will look distinguished, even if, at first, my biscuit making may be mediocre."

Beginning with a simple shortcake, which she could nibble with her sherry, she followed, more successfully than she had hoped, these recipes:

SHORTCAKE

Put three ounces of butter or margarine into a mixing bowl and stand it in hot water to become soft with two ounces of caster sugar. Mix it with a strong fork until it looks as pale and soft as cream, adding a little milk.

Sift into a dry basin four ounces of white flour and a half teaspoonful of salt. Sift this into the cream, mixing it evenly until it becomes a stiff dough. Dredge flour on a tray or whitewood table-top; put the dough on that, flour the top of it, flour the rolling pin and roll it out—about an eighth of an inch thick or more—and lift it on to a greased and lightly floured baking tin. Cut it into biscuit shapes while it is on the tin, and bake it in a low to moderate oven, say 350° F. (Mark 4 Gas), until it becomes *light yellow*. Spread fine sugar on top before cooking, to make it shine.

The centre of the oven is the best place to put the baking tin, where the heat is even and where the hot air can circulate freely.

Biscuits should never be left until they become brown or they will be very overcooked.

They should be lifted off the baking tin, inverted over a wire mesh and left to become crisp as the moisture evaporates.

RICE BISCUITS

Leave three ounces of margarine with three ounces of sugar in a mixing basin over hot water to soften while you sift four ounces of flour, and half a teaspoonful of salt with an ounce of ground rice. The ground rice gives a very "short" (brittle) texture. Sift this into the margarine-sugar, which has been creamed as for the shortcakes, and mix it thoroughly. Roll out the dough thinly on to a floured board or table. Cut into squares or rounds with a pastry cutter dipped in flour and lift them on to a greased, floured, thin baking tin. Bake them at 400° F. (Mark 6) for 10 to 15 minutes in the middle of the oven.

RICH NUT BISCUITS

Make a cream with three ounces of butter, three ounces of sugar and three drops of vanilla essence. Drop into it a fresh egg and beat it with a lifting movement to keep it airy.

Sift five ounces of self-raising flour, with half a teaspoonful of salt, and sift this into the egg-cream, making a soft, malleable dough. Roll it out, a clump at a time on a floured board. Shake over the top some chopped nuts—brazil, walnuts or almonds, rolling them lightly into the dough. Lift this on to the baking tin and mark it into strips with a sharp-pointed knife before baking at a low to moderate heat for about twenty minutes. The greater the proportion of fat to flour, the lower should be the temperature of the oven.

Meantime, roll out another clump of dough and shake

over it some desiccated coconut, rolling that in so that it sticks, and bake it in exactly the same way as the other nut biscuits.

When they are cooked, lift them on to an airy wire mesh nutty side up, to let them dry off.

ALMOND BISCUITS

Allow two ounces of butter and two ounces of sugar to melt in a basin with four drops of almond essence. Cream it with a fork; stir in two ounces of ground almonds and two tablespoonfuls of milk.

Drain the white out of an egg and whisk it stiff. Mix the yolk into the almond cream. Sift two ounces of self-raising flour with half a teaspoonful of salt. Sift it into the cream, lifting it gently until it is well assimilated. Spoon in the egg white and mix gently to keep it frothy.

The oven should be at 350° F. (Mark 4 for Gas) before these are put in. Take a teaspoonful at a time and drop it on to a thin, greased baking tin. Let it spread, and allow room for that when placing the next teaspoonful.

Decorate them if you like with a snippet of whatever crystallized fruit you may have—angelica, cherry, pineapple or apricot—just one in the centre while the frothy dough is moist. Try baking them on edible rice paper.

Shake a little caster sugar over the biscuits before baking to give them a *glistening effect* when cooked.

In fifteen minutes or less they should be cooked, so lift them on to a wire grill with a flexible knife and leave them to evaporate and become crisp.

When they are quite cold, put the biscuits into an air-tight tin, *to store.*

If they become limp through exposure to air, *re-crisp* them for a minute in a hot oven.

PASTRY IN ADVANCE

"I'm not going to start making pastry at this hour of the evening," said the Career Woman.

"But what if you had had the forethought to prepare it in advance?" asked her friend.

And it was that idea which exorcized that inhibition. When she was fed and rested, and gossiping perhaps, she sifted eight ounces of flour with a teaspoonful of salt, and sifted it again into a basin. Taking four ounces of margarine which had become very hard on her stone floor slab, she grated it into the flour, mixing it lightly with a fork until it was well blended and crumbly.

She scooped this into an earthenware crock and covered it with paper gripped with an elastic band and left it on the cold stone. This was the basic mixture to be made into SHORTCRUST, and it would keep fresh for a week.

PASTRY CASES

Another evening she would make the pastry. Taking out about four ounces of the dry pastry mixture, she mixed in a spoonful of sugar and just enough cold water to make a stiff dough, which she then rolled out on a floured board, beginning at the centre and *rolling outwards*, just once.

Cutting rings with a floured pastry cutter, she fitted

them into lightly greased and floured patty tins which she put into the oven at 400° F. (Gas No. 6) to be baked light yellow in about fifteen minutes. As some were to be re-baked on a future occasion on no account were those left to become brown.

Inverting the baked pastry cases on a grill to evaporate, they could be stored when cold, one inside the other in a tin.

FRUIT TARTS

In this way she could fill a pastry case with some stewed fruit, top it with cream (if any) and she had a cold sweet course in half a minute.

If her oven was in use, she could re-heat the pastry with its filling—apple, pear, plum, blackcurrant—stewed in advance, or jam if there were no fruit ready.

She might want to have the tart made hot even though the oven was not lit. In that case she filled the pastry case, or two, set them in a saucepan over moderate heat with the lid on and when they were hot right through they tasted as if they were freshly cooked.

She was rather pleased with the way in which she had managed her career and her domestic interests. "Soon", she said, stretching out in her arm-chair and lighting a cigarette, "I shall adventure into a little entertaining. That will be the time when I shall have to be quite resolute about the washing up last thing at night. Nothing would stultify me more than having to clear the kitchen before making my breakfast. It has been easy enough up to now while I have been feeding quite alone."

VIII

THE CONVALESCENT

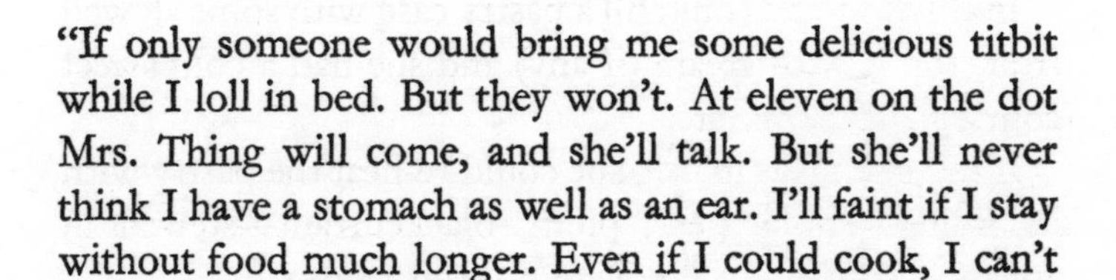

"If only someone would bring me some delicious titbit while I loll in bed. But they won't. At eleven on the dot Mrs. Thing will come, and she'll talk. But she'll never think I have a stomach as well as an ear. I'll faint if I stay without food much longer. Even if I could cook, I can't shop. What shall I do . . . ? If I go into the kitchen I shall begin sneezing again. Oh dear."

Presently the rattle and clang of the milk bottles proclaimed their arrival. "Ah!" she said. "At least I can drink fresh milk." And, wrapping herself around with a woollen dressing-gown, she brought in the milk, poured out a glassful at once and drank it. "That's better! And how easy!"

She opened her cupboard to see what food was there, and it was not as bare as she had thought: butter was there, cornflakes, oatflakes, an unopened, wax-paper-wrapped packet of crisp-bread, rice, cheese, eggs, oranges, lemons and dried fruits. Tins, too, but she would leave those while she was convalescing. "Better to have fresh food only," she thought. "I can begin building up on eggs. I wish I had a high stool so that I could sit as I scramble an egg," which she did, very simply, in five minutes.

SCRAMBLED EGG

Into a little fireproof dish over moderate heat she put about a tablespoonful of milk, a brazil nut size of butter, a shake of white pepper and salt.

While it was becoming hot, she held an egg against the light to see if any shone through. This is known professionally as *candling*. If it looks black it is a bad egg. If the light shines through it is good, though it may be stale. It is best to crack it open on a saucer, just in case!

Sliding the egg on the dish, it is then jabbed in the middle to break it up. A bone egg-spoon or a stainless flexible knife will do for the scrambling. It is simply scraped from the dish as it cooks. The uncooked egg falls into its place and, in a few minutes of scraping, or lifting, the egg is cooked. Buttery, creamy-soft, slightly savoury, it is a good beginning to stimulate the gastric juices which indicate a healthy hunger.

APPLE AND CHEESE

Later on she ate an apple with silver-paper-wrapped cream cheese, which keeps fresh for a week or more. A bite of each at a time modifies the sharpest apple, which, of course, is rich in the essential vitamin C.

Mrs. Thing came in later, bringing with her an astounding surprise—a little bottle of rum—"Not that I believe in solitary drinking, my dear, but there's nothing like egg-flip with rum to set you on your feet." So, once a day, she made variants of this combination, which made her pleasantly drowsy and relaxed for her afternoon rest. "How nice people are", she mused, "when one is sick."

EGG–RUM FLIP

A fresh egg is beaten up with a pinch of salt in a basin until it is frothy. Then it must be strained (through muslin preferably) into a tumbler. A teaspoonful or more of sugar will give it adequate sweetness for most palates. About a dessertspoonful of lime juice gives it a particularly pleasant piquancy which will offset the stickiness of the egg, and when the rum is added the flavour is deepened most satisfyingly. The amount of rum depends on many factors, but a dessertspoonful may be enough.

EGG AND MILK FLIP, WITH RUM

The egg is beaten up with a fork or whisked, but always, for the fastidious palate, the little globules (the potential life) must be strained away.

The milk added to the strained egg may be hot or cold, and a good whisk makes it so nice and light and frothy. Stir in any sugar, and finally, *after* whisking (not to waste any), the rum is stirred in. The hot milk is sleep-inducing, so it is a good drink to take in bed.

No lemon or lime should be added to any milk drink as it will curdle it.

EGG-MILK-RUM JELLY

A small saucepan and a little dish, a spoon and a fork is all the washing up to be done for this.

A teacupful of cold milk and a dessertspoonful of isinglass are stirred with a fork over gentle heat until the isinglass is melted. While it is hot but not boiling, a level dessertspoonful of sugar is added and, away from the heat, a fresh egg and a teaspoonful of rum. Beat this all up with the fork, pour it into a dish, and leave it in a cold place to set.

Whisking would make the egg thin, whereas the fork beating will leave it thick enough to set.

EGG-MILK JUNKET

This is made exactly like the egg-milk-rum jelly, but finally, when it has cooled to blood heat—warm not hot—(try the fork against the wrist) stir into the milk half a teaspoonful of liquid rennet. Vary the flavouring—almond, banana, rum, raspberry, orange or vanilla. Leave it to clot for ten minutes.

It is important to know that only fresh milk will clot, so never attempt anything else such as condensed or sterilized milk when making junket.

The egg is not necessary for making junket, nor the isinglass which congeals it. But by using isinglass or jelly powder, the watery substance from the milk—the whey—is fixed in it, instead of separating. The rennet (or junket powder) which clots the milk into a junket, sets the egg in ten minutes, so that one need not wait until the jelly sets before eating it. It is the quickest way to make an EGG CUSTARD, and it contains the added nutriment of the isinglass as well as being partly pre-digested by the clotting.

JUNKET

How quick it is to make an ordinary milk junket—enough for twice—with half a pint of milk made warm in a saucepan with a dessertspoonful of sugar. A few drops of flavouring essence and a teaspoonful of liquid rennet are then stirred in for half a minute, but not whisked. It must be poured immediately into the glasses or dishes from which it is to be eaten.

Any freezing must be postponed until after the clotting, which takes about ten minutes. Any decorative morsels such as finely chopped nuts (ground almonds are good), snippets of cherry, angelica or a crystallized violet must also wait for the clotting to take place.

The RENNET, whether in liquid or powder form, does not last indefinitely, but provided the container is kept tightly closed, after using some from it at intervals, it should retain its power for a few months.

EGG-RUM FROTH

As the convalescence proceeds one can spare some energy for egg whisking. The first reward might be this delicacy.

After straining the white out of an egg, whisk it until it is like stiff snow. Mix the yoke and half of the whisked white with a teaspoonful of sugar and another of rum, in a small dish or custard glass. Spoon the rest of the egg froth over it, shake caster sugar over that and leave it in a very cold place—preferably in a refrigerator—to become quite cold before eating it.

EGG CUSTARD

An egg custard will take half an hour to become set, in a basin surrounded by boiling water. Beat up an egg with a pinch of salt and a dessertspoonful of sugar in a small basin, while you bring a third of a pint of milk to the boil. Pour this on to the beaten egg, stir and then mix in the flavouring. Grated lemon rind (not the juice which would curdle the milk), grated orange rind, vanilla, almond—two or three drops only—are especially suitable to egg custard.

Bring about a pint of water to the boil in a saucepan and set the basin of egg custard in it, seeing that the water comes up as high as the custard. Put a saucer on the basin, put a lid on the saucepan, and let it *simmer* for about half an hour. Test the custard to see that it is quite set, by inserting a knife right through. If the knife comes away clean, it is cooked. Take the saucer from the top so that the cooling steam will not fall in drops of water over the custard and so spoil it. If the water around boils fast, the custard will become bubbly and hard.

CRÊME CARAMEL

The same quantities will make two or three mounds of crême caramel. Mix one egg with a pinch of salt and a dessertspoonful of sugar while a third of a pint of milk is brought just to the boil. But in this case use evaporated milk, or, preferably thin cream. Pour it on to the egg and stir, adding the flavouring. Pour this into little moulds, cover each with a lid—possibly a tin lid or a covering of tinfoil—set them in a saucepan of boiling water, as before, covering that with a plate or lid. These custards, being smaller, should set in about twenty minutes or less.

THE CARAMEL is made like this. A spoonful of sugar is put on a cooking plate over moderate heat. Move the sugar around with a wooden spoon or flexible knife until it is quite melted. At that moment it may begin to burn almost at once, so watch it carefully. Just as it is beginning to darken, add a teaspoonful of water, draw it from the heat and mix it quickly.

The cooked egg custards are loosened from their cups (or moulds) by running a knife around inside each, then inverted over the caramel which is spooned over the top.

The crême caramels should be eaten immediately, or kept hot until one is ready to eat them. Otherwise leave them to become quite cold.

A busy, provident person who likes this dish very much can make a quantity of this caramel (burnt sugar) at a time with a few ounces of sugar and a tablespoonful of water. Poured into a bottle and tightly corked, this will keep for weeks in good condition.

CHEESE EGG SOUFFLÉ

This is made like an egg custard, which is much easier than the soufflé proper.

A clove of garlic is crushed in a basin, to which is added an egg and half a teaspoonful each of salt and dry mustard with a shake of cayenne pepper. Beat this up while half a pint of milk is brought to the boil, which is at once poured over the egg and stirred. Mix in half a cupful of breadcrumbs and grate into it an ounce or two of cheese.

The basin, covered with a saucer, is put into a saucepan containing boiling water, and, with the lid on, it is left to simmer until the soufflé is set.

To save bother, use oatflakes instead of breadcrumbs.

POACHED EGG WITH CHEESE

This requires almost no mental effort to do. A fireproof saucer-plate is put over a low heat. Put in it a pat of butter, a spoonful of milk, some pepper and salt. When it is hot, slide the egg in; slice cream cheese over the top and cover it with a saucer.

In three to six minutes—depending upon whether one likes the white of the egg transparent or opaque—the egg will be set and the cheese melted. It is then ready to eat from its cooking plate.

FRESH FROZEN VEGETABLES

"Now is the time for a little steamed fish, plaice, turbot, smoked haddock with a poached egg on it, and some fresh, green vegetables. But if I can (and I will) go shopping—just a little journey—I can buy some FRESH FROZEN VEGETABLES. I like best the spinach and the garden peas."

These, in fact, need no preparation and almost no cooking. Taken out of their packet, they can be put straight into an open saucepan over the gentlest heat to let the ice thaw out of them, or simply left until that happens. Salted and peppered (a teaspoonful of sugar and a pinch of dried mint for the peas perhaps) and with a lump of butter added, they need only be heated right through over moderate heat. They are then ready to eat and they are always delicious.

FRESH FROZEN FRUITS

"To-morrow", she said, "I'll buy some FRESH FROZEN RASPBERRIES and let them thaw, and I'll eat them sprinkled with caster sugar and a great blob of cream on them. And the day after that I'll buy the BLACKCURRANTS and I might make a tart. And by that time I shall be convalescent no longer.

"But what I am forgetting, of course, is that I shall not eat the whole packet of raspberries at once. And once they are thawed they cannot be re-frozen. Therefore I shall put them in a glass jar—a wide one—with a screw top, pour castor sugar over them and a dessertspoonful of brandy, and screw the top down.

"Thank goodness one can buy the tiny sample bottles of spirits and liqueurs. One can have variety with these little extravagances without being involved in financial commitments or the storage problem. When I'm well off and have a huge apartment it will be different."

BRANDY CHERRIES

"I'll get a wee nip of the cherry brandy, too, for the frozen cherries, and one to keep until the fresh cherries come in. I'll halve them—the large, black ones, and pot them for a few days with a spoonful of cherry brandy."

COINTREAU ORANGES

"I'll pot orange slices with cointreau, too. And a little sugar to give them the sweetness they need."

KIRSCH STRAWBERRIES

"There's nothing like kirsch with fresh strawberries. Mixed with the cream or with the fruit. I could mix it with the thawed strawberries after pouring the water off. I'll get a packet right away. And a sample of kirsch. How easy it is to be experimental, even with limited resources and though quite alone."

The Convalescent

MILKY TEA

"Supposing, for instance, I make myself some milky tea? Why shouldn't I infuse it with boiling milk instead of water? It will do me more good. . . ." And thereupon she made the teapot very hot, put into it a dessertspoonful of tea and poured over that half a pint of boiling milk. Leaving it to stand for three minutes, she gave it a good stir, and strained it into her cup. She enjoyed it a lot. She felt stimulated. It was a success.

MUTTON CHOP

She thought she smelled a mutton chop being cooked. "Ah, . . . with chopped raw onion on top; it just softens a little while the chop is grilling; and the fat runs off, and the edge of fat is crisp outside and succulent within. . . . I'll buy one for myself! Quickly, before that person downstairs makes the whole place reek. She always cooks with a blazing heat. . . . I'll take the air. It will freshen me. I think—in fact, I believe—my convalescence is over."

IX

THE SCHOOLBOY MOOCHER AND THE STUDENT

"Have they really gone?" he called out to his sister.

She, watching out of the window, waved her final good-bye. It was always like that, saying, "Have a nice time," and the return for the forgotten umbrella, "Kiss good-bye again", and another return for keys, for a cheque-book, for an extra wrap. Even if it were only for a day, the commotion was as much as if they were going to America.

"Yes," she said, "Mother has squeezed herself into the old mobile parlour—she'll not get out of it now, and Father has slammed the door."

"Mouse-trap, I call it!" he said. "When I'm of age I'll have a really smart affair. I'll run you around sometimes, perhaps."

"They're off!" she said. "Get the saucepan out, and the sugar, and the butter, and the milk. Oh, better not use the butter. They'd notice it."

"We'll eat Margery on our bread, and smother it with fish paste or something. But we must have butter for the toffee to-day. It's almost my birthday."

"Let's make a lot so that I can take some back to my digs," she said, thinking of the comfort it was to chew some toffees while she did her solitary evening studies.

So they stood a strong saucepan over moderate heat, put in half a teacupful of water and a pound of sugar, and stirred it with a flat-ended wooden spoon until the sugar was quite dissolved. "Can't have it gritty," he said. Next they poured in about a quarter of a pound of golden syrup, a teaspoonful of salt, and nearly two ounces of butter. This was stirred continuously, even after it boiled. When it had been boiling ten minutes, they decided to test it, lifting the stirring spoon out and letting a small drop drop into a cup of cold water.

"Pour the water off and feel the blob," he said.

"It isn't a blob. It's a stream."

"Then we must cook for five minutes more," when they tested again.

"The blob feels almost firm," she said. "Rather like toffee when you've chewed it a bit."

"That means it's done. Hurry up and rub the tin over with butter on a piece of its paper, and we can scoop it on."

They used the shallow grilling pan which was large enough, and smoothed the toffee over the top with a flexible knife dipped in hot water. When it had set just firmly enough, they lifted it *en bloc* with an egg slice and turned it upside down on to well-buttered paper. "When it's nearly cool we can mark out the squares, and cut them through when it's quite cold," he said.

"I'll get the caramel papers which I've been saving up, and I'll wrap them so that they'll look like real caramels," she said. "But, of course, to make them especially chewy we should have used liquid glucose instead of the syrup. I'll buy some at the chemist, and hide it for the next chance we get."

"We forgot the flavouring," he said. "But it didn't matter since we had the butter. It's nicer plain when it's the real thing."

"We should have put the flavouring in at the very last stir, I know," she said. "A dessertspoonful of vanilla essence, a teaspoonful of almond essence, a tablespoonful of coffee essence."

"I like the COFFEE powder, but it takes an ounce for all this amount of toffee; or two ounces of cocoa to make CHOCOLATE TOFFEE, only we have to sift it in in case of lumps."

"What about nuts? Remember when we put the COCONUT in? We put so little we hardly noticed it. We could have used up to four ounces, easily. Shouldn't that be put in at the last stir, too?"

"Yes, and any other chopped nuts. By the way, let's crack some nuts and roast them. I'm strong in the wrist. You put the oven on."

And so she did, and when the nuts were cracked, the oven was hot enough to roast them. *Lightly* only, and with a number of shake-ups, to let the moisture evaporate. They were left to become cold before heaping them into paper bags and then into tins, so that they could be carried and stored cleanly for just that moment when nuts, almost more than anything else, can ward off that sinking feeling of hunger.

"Do they feed you well in your digs?" he asked his student sister.

"Not very. I always have to make up with oddments in my room. But I'm getting quite good at it. I have to have non-smelly things, though I keep cheese wrapped in silver paper, and I wrap the banana skins in newspaper until I get to a bin. I wallow in grapes, though."

"Oh, give me raisins every time; or sultanas. They're scrumptious with nuts."

"Let's make some FRUITY-NUTTY CAKES while we've got the oven," she suggested. "We've got the nuts and there's coconut in the cupboard, and condensed milk already opened."

"We won't use the roasted nuts. There's no need. I'll crack some more and you can chop them. A cupful will do, with a cupful of coconut and the same of sultanas and currants."

"And grated orange peel," she said, "it's nicer than candied peel, I think."

So they mixed all these things in a bowl and poured in enough condensed milk to make them stick. Then they teaspooned off the sticky lumps on to a margarined baking tin, and set it in the hot oven until the grand smell announced that the fruities were browned and crisp. They slid them out on to a grilling mesh, where they dried off finally, and those that were still uneaten when they were quite cold, they stored in a tin for future pleasure.

"I can make pikelets on my ring heater," she announced, "and pancakes, and bakestone cakes. But you have to have a thick frying-pan for that." And she showed him the recipes which guided her.

PIKELETS

Sift two heaped tablespoonfuls of flour into a basin. Add a large spoonful of fresh milk (though water will do) and stir until there are no lumps. Mix in another spoonful of milk, then a fresh egg and a good pinch of salt. Keep on beating this up with a fork until it is bubbly. This is *batter*, and it should be thick like clotted cream. Put the frying-pan on the heat and leave it until a nut of lard (or olive oil) in it is practically smoking hot. Pour a tablespoonful of the thick batter in the pan and watch it cook. In a few minutes, when it begins to bubble, lift the edge with a knife to see if it is brown underneath. If it is, turn it over and brown the other side. These can be eaten hot with butter, sugar and lemon juice; with honey, or with jam. If they are left to become cold, do toast them in front of the fire, both sides, before buttering them.

PANCAKES

Pancakes are mixed as the pikelets were, only the batter must run thinly. Only fresh milk should be used; enough to make it pour quickly. Powdered milk is no use; and it must all be kept stone cold. Margarine or butter sticks to the frying-pan, so nut-oil, olive oil or lard are the perfect things to fry pancakes in. Not too much, and it must be very hot or the batter will be grease-logged.

When pouring in the batter, only cover half the pan and twirl the pan to let the batter run all over it. Turning the pancake over is rather more tricky than with pikelets, which are smaller and thicker. The edge of the pancake should be crisp and rather frilly. They should be eaten at once, from a hot plate, with lots of sugar shaken on and some lemon juice, and rolled up.

BAKESTONE CAKES

Measure about four ounces of self-raising flour and sift it into a mixing bowl. (You can use a big saucepan.) Cut into it with a fork about two ounces of margarine, and go on mixing it until it all looks like breadcrumbs. Sift in half a teaspoonful of salt and two heaped tablespoonfuls of fine sugar, and mix it up. Flop in an egg (if you have one) and mix it smooth, adding enough milk to make a rather stiff dough. Use all milk if you have no egg. Mix in a handful of currants or sultanas, or chopped nuts and some chopped glacé cherries if you have any. Otherwise the cakes will have to be plain.

Flour a large plate, or a washable tray, and put a clump of the dough on it. Turn this over to flour the other side, and press it flat, to the thickness of not more than a quarter of an inch, with the back of a wooden spoon or a knife. Dip the edge of an inverted cup or glass into the flour and press it on the flattened dough to cut out ring shapes. Lift these on to a thick, hot, slightly-greased frying-pan, and let them become brown. Turn them over to become brown the other side. If the cakes are cut too thick, or the if pan is too hot, the insides will remain doughy—so you have been warned! Use up all the dough in this way, and each cake will be better than the last.

FLOUR DREDGER

One can make a simple flour dredger by punching small holes in the bottom of an empty cocoa tin, with a thin nail and a hammer. It stands upon its lid, therefore, which doesn't shake off.

"All that looks terribly professional to me," said her young brother, handing back her recipes unread.

"A professional wouldn't get far on that," she said, "but it's easy stuff for beginners, and it's wholesome. Some day I'm going to be a real cook. When I marry."

FRY-PAN CAKES

"I've just thought of something!" she exclaimed. "I think I can make proper cakes on a frying-pan."

"I'd like to see you do it," he taunted.

She took up the challenge, and did these things with great precision, getting two basins from the cupboard.

The one basin she stood in a bowl of hot water. She put

in it, to melt, two ounces of margarine and a heaped table-spoonful of fine sugar.

The other basin she left quite cold and drained into it the white of an egg, whisking it until it was stiff.

To the now melted margarine and sugar she added the egg yolk and mixed it up with a fork.

Then she put the frying-pan over moderate heat, with a tiny nut of margarine, to become hot. Sifting two heaped tablespoonfuls of self-raising flour with a small saltspoonful of salt into the egg-cream, she mixed it with the fork, making a smooth dough. Next she scooped into that the snowy white of egg, and mixed it *lightly* so as not to disintegrate the froth. There was no need of milk. The dough was just softly malleable, and so could be dropped, a forkful at a time, on to the hot, greased frying-pan, giving each blob a twirl with the fork to keep it round. Each little cake was about an inch and a half across.

She turned the heat rather low, and in five minutes or so the cakes had risen (there were six), and by lifting the edge she could see the underneath was becoming brown. In another minute she turned over each cake and let it brown on the other side. After which she lifted them off on to a wire grill to let the moisture evaporate.

When they had cooled a little, she bit one. It was crisp on the outside, of a fine airy texture inside, and cooked right through. Her brother watched her eat the whole cake, then tried one for himself. "Oh, I say! I'll have another," he was truly appreciative. "These are like fairy cakes, only softer; and lighter," he said. "And do you know, it's only half an hour since you first thought of it!"

COCONUT CAKES

Doing exactly the same thing again with the same measure of everything, she shook in, spreading it as she turned the fork, and at the last, just before the egg white, a dessertspoonful of desiccated coconut. These cakes rose at the first high heat of the pan, and became set as it was lowered, and then became brown on the other side when they were turned, as before.

WALNUT CAKES

Chopping up a few of the shelled walnuts, these were sprinkled on top of the cakes when they were just put on the pan. The moist softness of the dough held the nuts so that they settled. When the cakes were turned over, the nuts browned slightly with the cakes, and had that especially nice flavour of roasted nuts.

SULTANA CAKES

A level tablespoonful of cleaned and dried sultanas, mixed in, was another successful variation, which she tried later, as well as:

ALMOND CAKES

following the same basic method and measures, but mixing into the egg-cream a few spots of almond essence and a heaped dessertspoonful of ground almonds.

SAUCEPAN CAKES

She tried cooking the identical cakes in a hot saucepan, greased with a nut of margarine, as before. Putting the lid on kept the shape of the cakes more rounded, but they didn't rise quite as much. The lid collected moisture, so that, when she peeped to see how they were doing, she needed to wipe away the brown steam, replacing the lid after turning the cakes. It wasn't so easy to turn them in a deep pan, so, though the cakes were almost as good, they were a little less light than those done in the open frying-pan.

SAUCEPAN CAKE

"Now you're baffled," said her brother, and there was a taunting glint in his eye.

"Not yet," said she. "I'll try it another way. I'll mix a dough and put it in a tin in the saucepan. But it's got to have air circulating around the tin—that much I know—if only I had a little trivet or a perforated stand. . . ."

"What about a tin lid, with holes punched in it?" he said, and did it at once.

She had beginner's luck. She couldn't find a suitable tin, so used an ovenware basin; greased it well and floured it; poured in the cake mixture which reached two-thirds up the basin; which she stood on top of the perforated lid in the middle of the saucepan which was now quite hot. Putting the lid on the saucepan she turned the heat to moderate and didn't peep at it until fifteen minutes had elapsed. The cake had risen right over the top of the basin, but was still rather moist, so she wiped the lid and replaced it, leaving the cake to continue cooking for another five minutes.

The cake was very light and spongy. It was released from the basin by running a knife around it and letting it slide out on to a wire tray to evaporate.

It was only later she learned that a thin cake tin would have allowed the bottom of the cake to cook too quickly, and so become burnt before the top was cooked.

"We must let the saucepan cool itself gradually," he cautioned, "and the basin! Cold water on them at this moment would buckle the saucepan and split the glass. That's a scientific fact." So they didn't try to prove it.

SAUCEPAN BREAD

"Couldn't you make bread like that?" he said. "Then if you're short of bread one night . . ."

So she set about it at once. Sifting three ounces of self-raising flour into a basin with half a teaspoonful of salt, she sifted it again into another basin, adding to it a small tea-cupful of milk, mixing it into a soft but not soppy dough until it was perfectly smooth. Greasing the first basin well with margarine and dredging it lightly with flour, she scooped the dough into it, and left it to rise in the warmth while the saucepan became quite hot over moderate heat. She put in it the lid with the holes, and stood the basin on that, fitting the lid on the saucepan as before. In fifteen minutes the bread was nearly cooked, so she turned off the heat and left it to become light brown and crisp before taking it out, lifting it from its basin and standing it on an airy rack to evaporate. She was more proud of her little milk loaf than of her cakes, curiously enough.

"I feel equipped", she told herself, "for emergencies," and she felt, in a way, independent.

"Sister Anne, Sister Anne! Is there anybody coming?" he quoted from "Bluebeard". "Keep watch at the window while I get started, clearing up this Awful Mess before They come home."

"They won't be home for another hour," she said, looking at the clock. "But I'm starving. I need meat. Let's raid the pantry!"

"I'll tell you what I could do with, and that's *Port Flip*!"

"What on earth . . . ?"

"One of the boys says his family have it before they go shooting. They keep going for hours on it. It's port wine and egg."

"Shouldn't think they could shoot very straight on that."

"Worth trying, though, while the old man is out."

So they tiptoed (as if they could be heard) to the sideboard cupboard and got out the bottle. Then he beat up a fresh egg in a tumbler with a fork. "Better strain it," he said, pouring it through the tea-strainer into two tumblers —half each—and then poured port wine into each, stirring it well with the fork to make it slightly frothy. Putting the bottle safely away, they drank. "Rather queer!" they said to each other. But it produced a new sensation. "Watch me do the scissors step," he said. "I don't know if I'm light-headed or light-hearted," she said, but they both giggled a lot at nothing much and felt rather gloriously reckless.

X

THE LONELY MOTHER

(9 a.m. to 5 p.m.)

"They have gone!"

Every day of the week she felt that pang—one-third regret, one-third anxiety and one-third relief—as the children ran off down the hill to school. There they got their midday meal and would not be back for eight hours! One look at the kitchen piled high with used breakfast dishes was enough to dispel the pangs whatever they were. Her resolute attention was demanded.

Having had only a cup of tea to awaken her to the hustling activities of getting the children fed and away, her hunger mounted as the pile of dishes diminished, and she began to imagine the kind of breakfast she would cook for herself. While the washed dishes were dripping on their racks she would cook and eat calmly without developing the gnawing indigestion which comes from mental agitation.

She thought she would make a toasted snack, and, as the toaster-griller took nearly five minutes to become red-hot, she turned it on, began cutting the bread and looked in the larder to see what there was to choose from to grill over the bread when it was toasted.

COFFEE

Then she began to prepare her coffee. Putting the kettle to boil with a pint of water, she ground a heaped dessert-spoonful of coffee and put it into a small, wide jug which was being kept hot over the grilling plate. When the kettle was just boiling, she took it from the heat, filled a large breakfast cup with the boiling water, fitted in it a fine mesh strainer, putting a saucer over the top to keep everything hot. As the water now was just at the boil she poured a small cupful over the coffee grounds in the jug, stirred it briskly, and covered it with a lid. In one minute she stirred in the grounds floating on the top, gave it another brisk stir, and left it to settle for three or four minutes. Meantime she put on a half cupful of milk to become hot in a saucepan.

Emptying the hot water from the cup she poured the coffee into it through the strainer, and added the milk. As she sipped and inhaled the full-bodied flavour and aroma of the coffee, she told herself again, as so often before, that the care and precision of making coffee just right is well worth while.

CHEESE ON TOAST

Her bread was now toasted, and this day she had chosen a very simple mixture to be grilled over it, since she had a jar of breadcrumbs and a jar of grated cheese, which she had grated during odd intervals while she was cooking, and which she kept open to the air to avoid bluemould.

Mixing a spoonful of each in a basin with a pinch of dry mustard, a little salt and a drop of milk, she spread it over the toast and grilled it brown in half a minute.

GARLIC TOAST

On rare occasions she liked to cut a section of garlic over a piece of bread, butter it and then toast it. The children didn't care for it. It gives pleasure to the sophisticated eater, particularly when alone.

TOAST

Sometimes she liked DRY TOAST. The bread is cut thin and turned over several times during the toasting, then stood upright against a support to evaporate thoroughly. That is the time to butter it, so that the butter is not absorbed, or to eat it dry and crisp.

At other times she chose BUTTERED TOAST. The bread is cut thick, toasted at the highest heat, both sides, turning once only, to brown the surface and leave the middle soft. It is buttered while it is hot so that the butter soaks into it, and eaten at once.

When the toast is to be covered with a savoury, the flavour of margarine is overcome, so one can save the butter. "Though the present-day margarine is quite tolerable," she told herself, as she thought of the variety of things with which she might, on other occasions, cover her morning toast to make her breakfast snack, such as:

Poached egg	Fish paste
Scrambled egg	Meat paste
Sliced cheese	Tinned meat
Sliced boiled ham	Sliced tomato
Sliced grilled bacon	Sliced cucumber
Flaked fish	Pickled gherkins

or marmalade, which is surprisingly pleasant, put under the toaster-griller, as are all the other things, to become hot.

"I'll clean my house before I shop," she told herself, gathering up her dishes. "Who wants to shop first thing? Not I. There'll be plenty left by the time my work is done and I'm washed and properly dressed."

Since she wasn't tied to any time-table for all these hours she could eat when she chose and, as only her own tastes were to be thought of, what she chose. She could try out many of those herby, spicy dishes which the children might learn to love later.

She already had little glass jars containing ground coriander, mace, ginger, nutmeg and a pepper mill for allspice berries. She had celery seeds and fennel seeds, and dried basil, sage, mint, marjoram, bay leaves and cloves, as well as garlic. So she could experiment quite a lot with varying savours.

Also, she liked to try different kinds of cheese—Brie, Camembert (half boxes), Blue Vein, Gruyère, Dutch red, the Swiss cream cheese, the English lactic cheese—the Cheddar, Stilton and the Wensleydale—the strong and the mild, the milk and the cream, the processed without rind and the hardened Parmesan which she grated herself when she felt vigorous, to shake on soup as a condiment.

At times, held irresistibly by the intriguing names in the delicatessen shop which she passed, she would buy European garlic salami—a few ounces sliced thin as paper—or the Irish one tasting like the best ham compressed into this firm roly shape. Olives, black and green, anchovies, sweet-sour gherkins, black bread, tinned tomato paste, whole pimientos! All these fascinating things she liked to try, once in a while, alone. The children were inclined to reject them. The flavours were rather strong for their unspoiled (or undeveloped) palates, so she felt free to adventure with these things while they were at school.

Some days she would take her midday meal as late as 4 o'clock, and was newly fortified for the onrush of the children's arrival home, clamorously ravenous.

Yesterday, for instance, she had prepared for them a stew of lamb, and had taken her own portion out and eaten it in peace. She was then free to ladle out their portions, for which they each brought their plates in to the kitchen to be filled.

She followed this recipe, with occasional variations.

STEWED LAMB

A few pounds of the best end of the neck of lamb will provide a lot of succulent bones and such tender meat. The whole piece may be put into a large saucepan over moderate heat to allow the fat to melt somewhat while the vegetables are being scrubbed scrupulously in cold water—carrots and celery (the outer stalks cut across the grain)—the turnips or swedes and onions, peeled and sliced, as well as some tomatoes and possibly a cupful of lentils. All these will cook in the pot with the lamb, and although they will be overcooked and thereby lose some of their flavour it will have gone into the meat and the water. A pint of liquid should be enough, water or stock with tomato juice or apple juice and a spoonful of vinegar. The milder herbs such as marjoram or lemon thyme are best with lamb, or a pinch of thyme and one torn bay leaf.

When it comes to the boil, with a close lid on, it is turned to a simmer and the meat should be tender within an hour and a half.

MUTTON BROTH

Mutton, though leaner, is tougher than lamb and needs two hours to soften by stewing. Barley (soaked overnight) also takes about two hours of simmering to soften, so it is a suitable cereal to put in with mutton to make a nourishing broth.

Since there were so many occasions when it was impossible to gauge exactly how much the children would eat of what she had cooked for them, there was usually what they called "ends", the last of the dish, uneaten.

To avoid what might be a sorry sight on a large dish, she learned to put the remainder on to a small, fireproof dish, so that it could be dressed, ready to re-heat without unnecessary washing-up.

POTATO—AU GRATIN

Whatever boiled potato was left she liked to rub over a grater. This made it light and fluffy, easy to toast under the grill, with or without butter. Sometimes she scattered on it a grating of cheese as well.

FISH—AU GRATIN

Any white fish, flaked away from the bones and skinned while it was warm could be heated with butter, first over and then under the grill. A grating of potato over it before the grilling kept it from drying up. A covering of grated cheese over that, and grilled a golden brown, made a perfect meal with sliced tomato or gherkins around it.

MEAT—AU GRATIN

Any cooked meat, minced, needs a little onion or other savour to make it palatable the second time, she thought. The onion need not be cooked, provided it is chopped finely enough (but not grated which makes it mushy) before mixing with the meat. A tomato, finely sliced, moistens the meat, and it is kept so if potato is spread over it before the grilling.

COLD FISH

She was astonished to find how pleasant cold herring is, and cold plaice she grew to like more and more. (*See* p. 54.)

FRIED LOBSTER WITH RICE

Once when there was a portion of fresh lobster left she decided to make herself this delicious dish which she once had enjoyed at a very expensive restaurant.

She cooked half a cup of rice in a cupful of water and a little salt for twenty minutes (see page 39), and drew it to one side while she used a fireproof plate to fry the lobster very gently in a little butter, turning it over and over until it was hot right through. Giving it a shake of salt and cayenne pepper, she covered the lobster with the hot rice and turned on the grill. Next she cut over the rice several slices of the ripe cream cheese she had chosen, dotted it with capers and put it under the hot grill until the cheese was well melted and becoming brown. Meantime she cut up some watercress, sliced a fresh tomato and arranged it around the dish, which she bore to her dining-table in triumph. She ate it with such pleasure that she almost felt guilty the children were not there to share it.

She would make them something which they especially liked that very evening, to give them pleasure, too.

SAVOURY RICE WITH CHEESE

When there was a surplus portion of rice, she liked to mix it with a chopped raw onion and fry it gently in a knob of dripping. Adding some sliced olives and a topping of cream cheese or grated hard cheese, it was made golden brown under the grill.

RICE IN SOUP

The last spoonful of rice which hadn't been eaten at a meal she liked to put into a bowl of soup which she was going to eat that day. If the rice had gone dry (and it must be left uncovered to become dry or it will go sour) it had to be made soft again in the soup by letting it soak in it awhile, with a final simmer to make it hot.

THICKENING SOUPS

In fact, any thickening for soups should be done the day they are going to be used, because oatmeal, semolina (sprinkled in while the soup is fast boiling), noodles or any other of the macaroni shapes, rice or flour will go sour if kept more than a day once they are made wet.

So, when she made herself a portion of soup, taking the meat or vegetable juices from the large pot of broth or stew she was cooking for the children, she thickened just enough for herself. (*See* p. 125 for Roux).

She found that soups were strengthening and therefore reviving. Often a good bowl of soup with some bread would keep her going for quite a time when she was really in too great a hurry to stop for long, especially as a larger meal required a period of rest after it to digest it properly.

CREAM OF MUSHROOM SOUP

When there were mushrooms left over, in which case they would probably be already fried in butter, it simply meant chopping them small for the soup, which was thickened in this way.

A spoonful of cornflour is mixed to a paste with a small drop of *cold* water in a saucepan. When all the lumps are smoothed out, more water may be added, but preferably vegetable stock. After mixing that, a cup of milk is then added with pepper, salt and the chopped, buttery mushrooms. When it boils (it must be stirred fast all the time) the flour will thicken at once, and in a minute after that it will be ready.

Chopped watercress added at the last is particularly nice with mushroom soup.

CREAM OF CELERY, ARTICHOKE, ONION AND POTATO SOUPS

Alternatively a cream soup may be made from a WHITE ROUX base. Allow about a dessertspoonful of cornflour or plain flour to a pint of liquid. (Half pint for sauces.)

The flour is put into a saucepan containing an ounce of melted butter (margarine) or white dripping. It will sizzle, but it should be taken from the heat before it changes colour. When it is cold, just enough cold milk is stirred in to make a smooth paste. The rest of the milk is added gradually and brought to the boil over moderate heat, stirring all the time. In a minute after that it will thicken.

That is the time to mix into it any of the above white vegetables—cooked soft and rubbed through a sieve with a wooden spoon or the bottom of a basin—as well as pepper and salt.

CREAM OF TOMATO

This must be made with a white roux as above, but with vegetable stock or water and sieved tomatoes. The milk or cream, which would curdle if boiled with tomato, must be added at the last, or to the plate of hot soup to cool it.

MEAT SOUP

This seems to demand a brown colour to match the flavour. A BROWN ROUX base must be carefully done, but it is simple. A spoonful of flour is put into a hot saucepan containing melted dripping. The flour will sizzle and become fried brown in a minute, so it must be taken from the heat as it does it. A drop of hot water may be added to it if it is still hot, but if the flour has become cold, cold water only may be added—just a drop to mix it to a smooth paste before adding more liquid—*hot to hot*, or *cold to cold*—mixing it smooth before bringing it to the boil.

For meat soup the liquid must be meat juices or water mixed with potted meat extract, and, if possible, some small bits of meat. There may be the remains of a tin of meat, or the last of a joint of beef or mutton. This has to be simmered, immersed in water or stock, for hours to release the meat from the bones and extract the marrow from the bones themselves.

Any remains of cooked root vegetables enrich a meat

soup, especially when cut in tiny dice, or grated in over a coarse grater. Some finely chopped parsley or celery leaves is good with this, mixed in at the very last.

FRANKFÜRTER EGG

If there was just one remaining sausage, she augmented it by improvising a kind of omelette. Or she might buy a pair of the smoky Franükfrter sausages, and cut them in slices, slantwise.

With a little lump of lard in the hot frying-pan, she would break in an egg, move it around with a fork to break it up, then drop in the sausage slices, covering the pan with a plate. In a very few minutes the sausages would be heated through and the egg set. The covering plate from which she would eat being also hot, it was all very orderly and quick.

TINNED FRUIT

She always found it cold comfort to eat what was left over from a tin of fruit. But if it were made hot its character was changed for the better.

It seemed to need more sugar even if it were a sweet fruit, so with a spoonful over it, sometimes with a little jam over the top, it was made hot all through in a covered dish. Cooking it a little longer with the lid off to let the surplus moisture evaporate, it attained a syrupy effect and a richer flavour. A little cream and a sweet wafer biscuit made it perfect.

FOOLS

When there was a small portion of stewed fruit left over she sieved it, making a purée. Mixing this with a little extra sugar or honey in a sundae cup, she stirred into it a large spoonful of cream or evaporated milk and left it to become stone cold. For a yet undiscovered reason she, like everyone else, called these dishes, "fools"—BLACKCURRANT, GOOSEBERRY, RHUBARB, APPLE, PLUM.

Sometimes she made the remaining fruit into a jelly (recipe, page 79).

FRUIT WITH MEAT

Any of the sharper fruits such as pineapple, apples, plums or gooseberries she liked to slice, especially if they were uncooked, and arrange them around a little meat dish which she was re-heating by frying or grilling.

FRUIT IN VEGETABLE SALADS

She discovered how pleasant sliced apple, orange, banana and gooseberries are in a salad with chopped onion and lettuce heart. She liked mayonnaise on it, and when she was making cakes and had a use for an extra white of an egg, she made herself mayonnaise from the yolk. She kept it from drying up by pouring on it in its shell a tiny drop of salad oil.

MAYONNAISE FOR ONE

The egg yolk is put into a small basin or large cup (to save waste) with its own measure of cream. Evaporated milk is good for this. A half-level teaspoonful each of salt, dry mustard and sugar are mixed in well with a fork, and a good shake of pepper. Drop by drop a dessertspoonful of warm olive oil is mixed in thoroughly, and, lastly, a tablespoonful of vinegar.

On different occasions she gave the mayonnaise colour and a new character by adding a few sliced olives; a little piece of pimiento chopped; a few capers; a clove of garlic crushed; or some green pea purée with chopped water-cress.

Mayonnaise will keep for several days, but it should be covered tightly to keep it fluid.

TEA FOR ONE

"Now", she said, "I'll make myself a cup of tea."

There were several colourful tins containing different kinds of tea—Indian, China, Ceylon, Darjeeling, the smoky Lap Sang Soo Chong, Orange Pekoe, Earl Grey's perfumed with dried blossoms—all tightly closed to prevent loss of aroma by letting in the air. She liked to infuse a different one each day. It was interesting and kept her palate aware.

She didn't always want to make a pot of tea, but only one cup, and she saved herself a lot of bother by making it this way. Having put the kettle on and chosen the tea she wanted, she stood the jug containing a small amount of milk in a bowl of hot water. Stone-cold milk spoiled the tea, and hot milk made it skimmy.

When the kettle was nearly boiling she poured some of the water into her empty teacup, in which she had placed a *deep* tea-strainer, to make both hot. When the kettle was boiling and the steam pouring out steadily, she threw the water in the cup away, put a heaped teaspoonful of tea in the strainer, then poured boiling water on it to fill the cup, covering it with a saucer. In three minutes she lifted off the saucer and the strainer, and the tea was ready for the warm milk.

As she sipped, she reflected on the reluctance she often felt to eat at all. She recalled the days when she was too busy to think; when she worked until she felt like dropping, forgetful until that moment that she had scarcely eaten all day. "There are people in prison camps who are made to work without food. I'm behaving at such times like a captive with a cruel taskmaster. And I have no taskmaster, except Time. And what will Time do for me? Only give me wrinkles and sagging cheeks!

"So if I'm not a captive, and not a nun under a vow of abstinence, then why don't I give myself the pleasure of eating? Silence and solitude are imposed on me for many hours each day, but I needn't starve. I'm not poor. And yet there are days when I do! And I'm not the only one. . . . I must be a little cracked.

"But if I were expecting someone for lunch, or tea, I'd soon hustle myself and get something I know they'd enjoy. And I'd enjoy it, too. I always do when there's the incentive.

"Supposing then . . . let me imagine that someone is coming at midday, or at two or three, and that they will say they have not yet had their meal. Let me look in my cupboard, in the pantry and in the refrigerator, and see what is there. Then I'll imagine what I'd make, and write out a little menu.

"Why shouldn't I eat that menu? The things on it . . . ? I'll begin now; and turn over a new leaf."

INDEX

Index

Index

Index

Index

Index

Index